HOW TO IMPROVE
CONCENTRATION

ADVANCE PRAISE

'Knowledge is the piling up of facts, wisdom is simplifying it! Quietly and wisely, the authors make a perfect case for dumping the din of modern ways and practising new simple techniques to master the ancient art of concentration. Practical advice is sprinkled throughout. "Disconnect to reconnect better" is one of the key messages that the authors nicely put across. It is a must-read treasure for anyone and a gem for any library. After all, old ways don't open new doors'—Dr Mohit D. Gupta, professor of cardiology, G.B. Pant Institute of Postgraduate Medical Education and Research

'The authors combine their years of passion and experience, working with learners of all ages, with the ageless wisdom of how to channelize innate human strength towards self-progress. The book makes for a good and practical read for adults as well as youngsters in their journey towards self-improvement. The authors also remind us of our everyday vocabulary that we take for granted, as it holds a much deeper significance in our lives. "So be careful while choosing whom and what you pay attention to . . ."'—Bhanu Prasad M.N., innovation and entrepreneurship coach, TCS Foundation

'*How to Improve Concentration*, as the illustration on the cover of the book suggests, takes you towards the core and the depths of your mind. The book would be extremely useful for readers of all ages who want to enhance this much-needed skill of concentration in these highly distractible·times. The book would be very helpful in mastering this skill as it is written in a very engaging, reader-friendly and illustrative style'—Avdesh K. Sharma, consultant, well-being psychiatrist, chairperson, RAHAT Charitable and Medical Research Trust

HOW TO IMPROVE
CONCENTRATION

BY GUINNESS WORLD RECORD HOLDERS

ADITI SINGHAL AND
SUDHIR SINGHAL
WITH BALA KISHORE

EBURY
PRESS

An imprint of Penguin Random House

EBURY PRESS

USA | Canada | UK | Ireland | Australia
New Zealand | India | South Africa | China | Singapore

Ebury Press is part of the Penguin Random House group of companies
whose addresses can be found at global.penguinrandomhouse.com

Published by Penguin Random House India Pvt. Ltd
4th Floor, Capital Tower 1, MG Road,
Gurugram 122 002, Haryana, India

Penguin
Random House
India

First published in Ebury Press by Penguin Random House India 2020

Copyright © Aditi Singhal and Sudhir Singhal 2020
Foreword copyright © BK Shivani 2020

10 9 8 7 6 5 4 3 2

ISBN 9780143427520

Typeset in Minion Pro by Manipal Technologies Limited, Manipal

Printed at Repro India Limited

www.penguin.co.in

MIX
Paper from
responsible sources
FSC® C047271

To the
Almighty God,
the Supreme Father of all souls and
the source of true knowledge

Contents

Foreword

Om Shanti and greetings of peace.

Congratulations to Aditi Singhal, Sudhir Singhal and Bala Kishore for identifying such a pertinent topic and bringing out a valuable and interesting book to enhance concentration. All of their wealth of knowledge, subject-matter expertise and decades of experience are reflecting through these pages.

Learning to focus is the key. Whether at home, school, work or anywhere for that matter—holding our concentration for designated durations is a priceless quality. After all, our success is inseparably connected to our thoughts. But for many of us, it is a daily struggle to remain focused on whatever task is at hand, living as we do in times of unending distractions. As a result, we become anxious, overwhelmed and confused, and feel unproductive.

This book shows that achieving deep focus is not elusive after all. With systematic training of the mind, we can clear away distractions, concentrate our thoughts completely on a single idea or task, and accomplish everything with quality. The content is well researched and the chapters are filled with wisdom, insights, techniques, tips, recommendations, examples and exercises. The book explores mind-based practices, concentration techniques, memory-retention tips and meditation insights, and suggests several guidelines to enhance the capacity of our mind. The real-world applications are easy to read, understand and integrate in daily life.

I am certain that this book shall teach us to successfully overcome personal barriers for concentration, and bring out the best in us. This is because it provides easy and innovative ways to overcome unsettled feelings about our long and never-ending 'To-Do' list. When we are stressed, angry, scared, upset, hurt or worried, we cannot concentrate. So every morning, we need an inner preparation to decide how we are going to be throughout the day in different scenarios, to successfully complete all that we need to do. Regular practice of meditation and indulging in a spiritual study in the morning purifies our thoughts and feelings, and declutters our mind, keeping it calm and stable. This increases concentration so that the mind focuses on one thing at a time. We will then be able to release mental clutter, cultivate discipline, stay focused, build momentum towards our goal, develop a positive mindset and become productive. In that sense, as we turn these pages, we turn our life in a positive direction.

BK Shivani

1

What Is Concentration

Concentration is a word that becomes a part of our life at an early age. As students, we are told by our parents and teachers to concentrate on our studies and acquire other skills. As adults, our bosses tell us to concentrate on our jobs. But is there anyone who teaches us *how to concentrate*?

We have asked this question to thousands of people, including students, teachers and parents in numerous workshops that we have conducted across the country. You will not be surprised by the answer. Almost everyone said *no*, even as every single person admitted to have always been told by their parents, teachers, bosses and others in their lives to concentrate on whatever they were doing.

Isn't it amazing?

We all know that concentration is very important in any kind of work we do, be it studies, driving, cooking, texting, etc. We often experience it in our daily lives, but very few of us understand exactly what it means or how to master it.

WHAT IS CONCENTRATION?

You will find different definitions of 'concentration' across sources. The most common ones are listed below.

- Concentration is focusing on one task at a time.
- It is controlling your mind at will.
- Concentration is a stage when you are taking interest in one task.
- *Ekagrata* is the Sanskrit word for concentration; it means giving prominence to only one (thought) in the midst of many (thoughts).

All of these are correct in their own way and in essence talk about the same idea. But as concentration is an intangible thing and has many different characteristics, let us try to understand it through the story of a scientist. There once was a man who was totally engrossed in an important research project. He spent days in his study, working on his research, completely neglecting his family members and other daily affairs. His wife understood the importance of his work and his behaviour did not bother her at first. In fact, she prepared his favourite dishes every day, taking the utmost care that they were cooked just the way he liked them. Days passed, but there was not a single word of appreciation from the scientist about the food his wife served him lovingly. After a month, the wife lost patience and decided she would start serving him food without salt. She thought this might catch the scientist's attention and he would at least complain about it. To her disappointment, the scientist ate the food without even noticing it was saltless. This went on for quite a few days.

One morning, just as the scientist took the first bite of the saltless breakfast served to him by his wife, he made a face and asked, 'Have you forgotten to add salt in my food?'

The wife looked at him, surprised, and asked, 'Are you done with your research?' The scientist said, 'Yes, late last night I completed my work and will submit it today. But how do you know?' The wife stood there with a mysterious smile on her face.

During the research, the scientist was totally engrossed in the task at hand. For him, nothing else mattered. This is an example of 100 per cent concentration. **Concentration is not just about focusing on one thing, but also about disconnecting from all the other things that might take away our attention from the task at hand.** Ignoring other things does not mean they are not important. It means those things are not our top priority at that moment.

Now, you might wonder: **In a world full of distractions and disturbances, is it possible to attain 100 per cent concentration on a single task?**

Yes, it's possible.

Look around you. You will see a child playing a game on a phone or a tablet with complete concentration. It's not difficult to find love-struck couples engrossed in conversation or just lost in each other's eyes, even in a fully packed bus or a metro coach. A person reading a book with full concentration and unaffected by the commotion around is not a rare sight.

Let's try finding a common thread in all the situations mentioned above. The lovers are lost in each other because of their *love*. Children play games on the gadgets because they *love* the thrill and excitement that the game brings, which come with attaining the highest scores. The scientist in the story related earlier was *passionate* about the completion of his research, which was his goal. The common thread here is the *love* for the task at hand. When you love something, your brain focuses all its power and attention on it. Hence you are able to automatically achieve the concentration you desire.

In order to have complete concentration,
you need to have love and passion for your task.

Observe the successful people around you, whether they are professionals, businessmen, students, sportspersons or homemakers. You will notice that they love doing their work. If you ask them how many hours they work, most of them will tell you that they lose track of time when they are working.

*How can we develop such concentration
in every task we do?*

THE SECRET TO ABSOLUTE CONCENTRATION

During one of my maths workshops, when I [Aditi Singhal] told the participants that I once created a national record, certified by *Limca Book of Records*, for fastest calculation (writing a times table of a 13-digit number in 1 minute 13 seconds), one of them asked me if I had been good at calculations ever since I was a child. Here is how that conversation went:

> 'I learnt the fast calculation techniques at a later stage in life and practised them to master the speed,' I answered his question.
>
> 'How long should I practise if I want to become like you?'
>
> 'About two hours every day.'
>
> 'If I practise for two hours every day for the next six months, will I be able to calculate as fast as you?' the participant asked curiously.
>
> 'Well, it all depends on you. You may take longer or you may even become better than me in that much time. But always keep one thing in mind—no matter how long you take, don't let go. Remember, practice makes perfect.'

If you practise something every day, you will surely become an expert at it one day. The keyword here is *practise*. Now just think of what you practise most often. **DISTRACTION**! Not just for two hours, but for about twelve to thirteen hours every day. All our waking hours, we practise distraction, and you will agree that we are getting better at it. We get distracted by even a slight knock on the door, even though we were engrossed in a very important task. We talk on the phone while cooking or driving, without caring about the consequences.

What should we practise instead? **CONCENTRATION**. You must remember two things about concentration:

- First, that it is a *skill*, and therefore has to be *learnt* and *practised.*
- Second, that it is a *wilful act* and cannot take place automatically. You should be willing to learn it. No one can teach you anything unless you yourself are willing to learn.

Let's do an activity to experience concentration:

> *Sit comfortably with your back straight and feet relaxed. Take a deep breath. Breathe slowly and deeply. Try to relax as you breathe. Now become consciously aware of the room around you, the chair you are sitting on. Now think about your birthdays over the years. Which one pops up in your mind? How did you celebrate it? What was the best birthday gift you received that day? Think about the person who gave you that gift. Who all were present at the time—your friends or family members? Think about how you felt at the time and try to relive those wonderful moments. Now become aware of the room again, become aware of the chair you are sitting on.*

You will of course remember the exact date of these memories as your birthday falls on the same day every year, but you might not remember the year. This is because we don't create memories in terms of days, months and years. Our memories are made of moments associated with particular thoughts, interests, emotions, people, places or events with which or with whom we were fully engaged. In the above activity, we led your conscious mind to one such moment of your life, and as a result, you were able to focus only on that moment. As you thought more about that moment, every detail became clearer in your mind. *That* is concentration: investing your thoughts, emotions and mental energies in one thing.

While performing the above activity, your thoughts might have wandered away from your birthday. For example, while visualizing a friend at the party, you might have remembered another moment or experience you shared with them, in the process taking your thoughts away from your birthday. When that happens, gently bring your attention back to your birthday. Bringing back the attention to the subject in focus is one of the important ways to improve your concentration. The more you pull your attention away from different distractions and focus on the task at hand, the easier it becomes for you to concentrate.

We face distractions every day of our lives and with every task that we do. We then spend all our energies in trying to keep our focus on the task at hand, but we also need to *detach* ourselves from the things that are diverting our attention from our work. Only then will we achieve full concentration.

Concentration is not just about connecting your mental and physical energies to one task,
but also about disconnecting from the things not relevant to the task.

Before you start learning how to improve your concentration, let's first test your concentration at the present moment. Some of the tests that can help you assess your concentration are given below. We recommend that you go through them before reading further.

Test 1: Do you see the hidden panda in the picture?

Test 2: There's a panda hidden between these elephants too. Can you find it?[1]

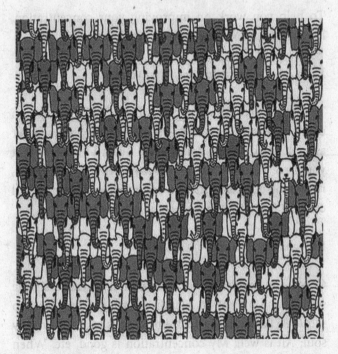

There are many other tests available online that can help you test your level of concentration.[2]

---

[1] For a complete set of such tests, visit https://www.mentalup.co/blog/concentration-test

[2] For more tests, visit https://www.psychologytoday.com/intl/tests/career/concentration-focus-skills-test

EXERCISES

To help you work on improving your concentration, here are some exercises you can start with.

Exercise 1 – *Counting with just your eyes*

Take any book and count the words in any one paragraph using only your eyes and without pointing your finger at each word. Then, count them again to be sure that you have counted them correctly. After a few times, repeat the exercise with two paragraphs. When you feel comfortable doing this much, do a whole page.

Exercise 2 – *Mental repetition*

Choose an inspiring word or phrase, or just a simple sound, and repeat it silently in your mind for two minutes. For example, I am a peaceful soul; I am a happy soul; All is well; My concentration is good, etc. When your mind can concentrate easily for two minutes, try to reach up to five minutes of uninterrupted concentration.

Exercise 3 – *Absolute focus*

Take a piece of paper and draw a small triangle, square or a circle, about three inches in height, and paint it with any colour of your choice. Put the paper with the drawing in front of you and concentrate on the shape you have drawn. For now, only the drawing exists for you and no unrelated thoughts or distractions. Keep your attention on the drawing and avoid thinking about anything else. Be careful not to strain your eyes.

Exercise 4 – Inner visualization

Draw a figure on a piece of paper, but after looking at the figure for a moment, close your eyes and visualize the figure in your mind. If you forget how the figure looks, open your eyes for a few seconds, look at the figure, and then close your eyes and continue with the exercise.

Exercise 5 – Open-eye visualization

This exercise is the same as Exercise 4 but with a little change. This time visualize the image you've drawn with your eyes open, looking away from the figure.

Answers to Test 1 and Test 2

How to Improve Concentration

2

Attention, Please!

What you register or experience is determined by what you pay attention to. Only the things we pay attention to seem real to us, whereas whatever we ignore—no matter how important it may be—seems to fade into insignificance. If you go to a shop looking for red shoes to match your red dress, your gaze will stop only at that colour and you will not notice other shoes, no matter how stylish they are.

WHAT IS ATTENTION?

Look around the room you are in. Observe all the white things in the room; it may be the paint on the wall, the clothes, the curtains, the fan, the switchboards, the furniture, etc. How many white things did you notice? Now without looking around again, can you recall the blue things in the same room? Look around again. You will notice that you missed many obvious blue things.

Because your first task was to look for the white objects, you ignored the rest of the colours present around you.

In spite of the visual stimulus, you did not allow it to register mentally. That's what attention does. It is like the beam of light from a torch in a dark room. You will be able to see only certain things in that light. The others remain invisible.

Therefore, here is how we could define attention:

Attention is the capacity to focus on one element or thing while ignoring all others.

Attention is a fantastic filter. What kind of information goes in and gets registered in our brains depends on what our attention allows in. And who regulates this filter? You! You are the master of your attention. You control your attention.

ATTENTION VS CONCENTRATION

Breathing and sleeping are the only activities that humans do without explicitly learning. Everything else is learnt by paying attention to what is being taught. **Attention** and **concentration** are two terms that are used interchangeably when we talk about learning, but are actually different.

If paying *attention* to something is, as discussed earlier, like a beam of light from a torch in the dark, then your choosing which object to throw light on is the act of *focusing*. Staying with that chosen object for a long time without getting distracted is *concentration*.

Concentration has to be directed only on one task, otherwise it will not have the desired result. It is inherently an act of exclusion. Concentration is thus the ability to pay selective attention to something while ignoring other things. It is the ability to control one's attention. We cannot concentrate on an object or an activity unless we pay selective attention to it. For example, a person trying to understand a mathematical concept needs to concentrate on it entirely, otherwise they will not be able to apply the concept correctly to the questions.

WHY IS PAYING ATTENTION IMPORTANT?

What we pay attention to and what we ignore shapes our moment-by-moment experience.

Attention and Learning

Learning is a combination of acquiring knowledge and also retaining it. You will be able to remember something only if it gets converted into a network of neural connections inside your brain. And attention is the key to the formation of these neural connections, called neural networks. Think of it like this: *Attention is the glue that helps 'stick' the information to your brain in the form of neural networks.* If there is a lack of attention while learning something new, you won't remember it for long. If while studying you are not focused or paying attention, you won't register what you read even if you spend hours working on it. This is because the information is not being stored in the form of new neural networks.

Attention and Relationships

How long can you speak to a person who is absorbed in their mobile and does not look at you while you speak? As human beings, we crave respect and attention from other human beings. All of us carry this large invisible tag around our neck that says 'Respect Me'. Most problems in relationships arise because of not paying attention to the other person, be it your friend, parent, spouse or child. Paying attention to the other person is the key to strong and healthy relationships.

(Source: Aruna Ladva, *It's Time . . . to Be Cool*,
London: BK Publications, 2016.)

It is very common in relationships that one partner wants to talk while the other one, involved in another activity, just pretends to be listening. They assure their partner by saying, 'Yes, I am listening. Carry on.' But actually, they are not listening, just hearing. Hearing is listening without attention.

Hearing + Attention = Listening

On the contrary, when you pay attention to the person who is talking to you, for those few minutes, you are essentially saying 'You are my world'. Your focus is only on them, and not on anything else. When you look into the eyes of the person speaking to you, you acknowledge their presence and feelings, and they feel respected and loved. That's how relationships are built.

Attention and Resilience

Failure is a part of life, and so are the feelings that stem from failure. But whether you learn from failures or get overwhelmed by them depends on what you choose to pay attention to. If you pay attention to the lessons you need to learn from your failure and not just the feelings of dejection or sadness that may emanate from it, you can become more resilient. But if you choose to indulge in these feelings, you may not gather the courage to try again. At the same time, it is also very important to acknowledge and not ignore these feelings. It helps to focus on becoming better next time and, in the process, also motivate yourself to work harder. If you ignore the lessons that need to be learnt and let the feelings overwhelm you, you would lose the motivation to keep trying and not develop the resilience you need as a life skill.

Attention and Quality of Life

Being attentive improves the quality of life. If you want to truly experience life, you should learn to focus and pay complete attention to what you're doing at any given moment. Try this the next time you sit down to eat something—put your mobile on silent and pay attention to the food in front of you. Observe the colour, texture, shape of the item in front of you; take in the aroma, and relish the taste as you gently take a bite. This kind of mindful eating enhances the experience of eating food. Similarly, when you are spending time with your family, remove all distractions and be present fully. A lot of our dissatisfaction is caused by our inability to pay attention to the task at hand and letting our attention drift to multiple other things. To enhance the quality of your experiences and thus the quality of your life, it is essential that you control this habit of drifting.

There are many thoughts that cloud your mind at any given time. It's up to you to choose which thoughts to pay attention to and which to ignore. Where do you want to direct your attention? That's what shapes one's existence and reality. At every moment, we are making a choice, and as a result, making our own reality. That's also how *habits* are formed. You pay attention to an action, repeat it, and it becomes easier with each attempt. In no time, it becomes a habit.

(Source: Aruna Ladva, *It's Time . . . to Be Cool*,
London: BK Publications, 2016.)

We all begin by *choosing* to check our mobile phones at every notification, paying attention to it every time it rings. Now that this has turned into a *habit*, we keep checking our phones even if there is no new notification. How often do we check our phones for the blue ticks after sending a WhatsApp message to someone? Once the ticks turn blue, we become restless again, waiting for a reply. This restlessness soon becomes a habit and seeps into other spheres of our life too. This is actually one of the major obstacles to achieving concentration.

If we want to change our habits, we need to check the kind of things we are paying attention to. We need to exercise our power to make a choice—the power to choose what is right for us.

WHAT DIVERTS YOUR ATTENTION?

Consider this scenario: A CEO receives an unexpected email from his marketing manager, asking for an appointment to speak about something important. His mind starts racing about what his manager is going to say. Is he going to ask for a raise? Is he going to resign? Does he have any complaints about his co-workers or the working conditions? The CEO wonders if he'd be able to manage if the manager leaves without serving the notice period? All these worries lead to a number of mistakes in the report he is preparing.

Similarly, while cooking, if you are not focused and your mind wanders, you may forget something as basic as adding salt to the dish.

There are many factors that take our attention away from a task at hand, thus leading to mistakes. These factors can be *external* or *internal* stimuli.

The factors mentioned in the above examples are **internal stimuli,** i.e., mental or emotional distractions that divert our attention towards irrelevant matters, creating stress.

Then, there are **external stimuli**. Imagine you're preparing for an important presentation and are totally engrossed in it. But there is a loud and constant noise coming from a celebration next door. You immediately get distracted and upset, and lose focus on the presentation. If your phone rings while you are driving, you immediately take your eyes off the road to see who is calling. These are external stimuli, i.e. external factors that demand our immediate attention. Letting external stimuli take over our attention can lead to serious consequences—in the above cases, giving a bad presentation at work and an accident, respectively.

Now, imagine a student sitting in a classroom taking keen interest in what is being taught by the teacher. His attention is suddenly diverted by the chirping of a little bird sitting on the window (external stimuli). The bird reminds him of the bird-print shirt that he wore to a party last night (internal stimuli). These thoughts take him miles away from the topic being discussed in the class.

DO NOT SLICE YOUR ATTENTION

When you rapidly switch your focus from one thing to the next, you are simply slicing your attention. Think of a situation where you're listening to a podcast or reading a book like this one. Suddenly, you get a text message and immediately start reading it. By the time you raise your head and come back to the book or the lecture, you won't have the same kind of focus as before. Imagine you are typing an email and suddenly a Facebook notification pops up. Even if you look at it only for a second before you go back to the mail, the little bit of diversion is enough to cut your attention by half. And when you try to do too many things at the same time, what you are effectively doing is *slicing* your attention, cutting it into pieces. When attention is broken into pieces, you no longer get the desired result from the activity you're performing. If these instances of slicing pile up, and it becomes a habit to divide your attention into pieces, it eventually starts affecting the way you perform in your personal and professional life. It can deter you from achieving your full potential.

> *Paying attention is like giving away a slice of your life.*
> *So be careful while choosing whom and what you pay*
> *attention to.*

On the one hand, we say we want to live life joyfully, we want to experience it, we want to learn, we want to grow, and on the other, we willingly divide our own attention without giving it fully to any one thing, and rob ourselves of our own experiences and joy. Technology is supposed to make our life easier, but we are enslaved by it. We are a generation that spends hours looking at what essentially is an object made of glass and metal, but cannot pay attention to any task for more than twenty minutes. We have a world of knowledge in our palm, but we spend most of our time paying attention to what's going on in the lives of other people. We click pictures to capture significant moments, but in that process, we forget to live the moment. There is an urgent need to check our addiction, and to bring our attention to more important matters than being on Instagram, Facebook and WhatsApp.

If you want to work and grow, the most important resource you need to safeguard is your attention. If you want to work and grow in the right direction, you need to drive your attention in the right direction.

Here are a few exercises that will help you keep your attention on the task at hand for longer durations. With practice, you will be able to effectively handle the external and internal stimuli that distract you from your work. These exercises are tried and tested and show great results.

EXERCISES TO IMPROVE YOUR ATTENTION

1. *I Am Here*: While reading a book or listening to someone speak, we tend to get distracted by even the slightest sound or movement, or our own thoughts. To bring our attention back, it helps to associate a phrase to it. For example, say 'I am here' to yourself when your attention moves away. This will immediately bring your focus back to the present moment and to your work. If your attention drifts off again, repeat the phrase. This exercise played a pivotal role in helping me [Aditi] create a national record for fastest calculation, mentioned earlier.

2. *No-Check Time*: Keep track of the number of times you look at your phone in an hour to check for messages or emails. Fix a period of time, like two or three hours, during which you will *not* check your phone or laptop or other gadgets. Don't worry about missing out on important communication as people can always call you or someone in your family in case of an emergency. This practice has helped

---

many of our students and loved ones control their urge to be online all the time.

3. *Mindful Me*: Mindfulness means paying full attention to what is happening around you and what you are doing. When you get up in the morning, sit in a comfortable place and use your five senses to be mindful of your surroundings. First, look around you and identify five things that were always there but you haven't noticed for a long time. They could be anything—a painting, a candle stand or a napkin holder.

Next, try and concentrate on the sounds around you. What all do you hear? Chirping of birds, cars honking, music . . .? How many sounds can you notice? Now let's come to smells. Which kinds of smells can you identify around you? The aroma of your morning tea or coffee, incense sticks, something being cooked in your kitchen or outside? Acknowledge all these smells.

Next is taste. Pay attention to the taste of tea, coffee or milk that you may be drinking. Is it sweet, bland or bitter? Concentrate on the flavour and texture in your mind.

The last one is your sense of touch. Concentrate on the different parts of your body. Start with your face or your arm. Feel the temperature—does it feel warm or cold? If you are holding something in your hand—perhaps a book?—how does it feel? Soft or hard? Pay attention to the chair you are sitting on. Is it cushioned or does it have a hard wooden surface?

Are your elbows on the table? How does it feel? Are your feet touching the floor? Does the floor feel cold against your feet? Or if you are sitting with your legs folded, do they feel numb?

If mindfulness becomes a part of your daily routine, it can bring sanity even to the most chaotic situations.

4. *The Spotlight*: We often get distracted while speaking to other people. To keep your attention from wandering, imagine a lit bulb over the head of the person you are speaking to. Even if you are speaking to someone on the phone, perhaps your partner, visualize their face with a bulb over their head. This practice can go great lengths in improving your attention, interactions and relationships.

5. *Attentive Listening:* Listening is the most important part of communication but also the most neglected one. Practising attentive listening goes a long way in increasing your attention span not just while talking to someone but in other areas too. As a rule, do not interrupt others while they are speaking. Just acknowledge what they are saying and allow them to finish. This not only helps us focus better on the content of the conversation but also improves interpersonal relationships. After all, good listeners are everyone's favourite.

Practising these exercises regularly will bring about a huge change in your life. It will increase your attention span and help you attain complete concentration.

3

Test Your Attention

Here are some interesting tests to ascertain your level of attention.

TEST 1[1]

In order to complete the test quickly, you must first go through the questions carefully. It's a very simple test. Your aim should be to complete it as fast as possible.

Let's start:

1. Without looking at your shirt, count the number of buttons on it.
2. How many zeroes are there in the number 10000000000086?
3. Circle this instruction.
4. How many '/' are there in the following pattern? \\\///\\\\///\\/\//\/////\\//

---

[1] Alan Chapman, Businessballs.com, 2016, https://www.businessballs.com/mental_concentration_test.pdf

5. Count the letter W in the group of letters given below:

   WMMWMMWMWWMWWMWWMM
   MMWMMMWMWWWWWWMWM
   MWMWWMMWWMMWWWMWMW
   MWWWMWWMMMWMWMWMW

6. Calculate the answer: $7 - 4 \times 2 + 3$

7. Count the number of vowels in the sentences given below:

   - Observation is a skill that takes time to hone.
   - Keep practising, even if you think you will never improve your concentration.

8. Draw a star on the upper-right corner of this page.

9. Convert these four numbers—6, 10, 13, 5—into letters using the coding given below and write the letters in the reverse order.

   $1=A, 2=B, 3=C$, and so on.

10. Now that you have finished reading all the questions carefully, do only question 4.

Solution

If you solved all the ten questions, we are sure the last one made you laugh. Just because you did not pay attention to the instructions given at the outset ('In order to complete the test quickly, you must **first** go through the questions carefully') you unnecessarily spent so much time and energy on tasks that weren't even required.

In case you read and followed the instructions carefully, and solved just question 4 to get the answer '18', then congratulations! You did have your attention focused solely on the test.

TEST 2[2]

Find the number of times the following words appear in the grid below to test your attention. The words are hidden and can appear horizontally, vertically, diagonally or backwards.

RUN, BUN, BONE

B	B	U	N	U	S	O	N
S	O	B	O	B	R	U	N
R	N	N	U	U	B	S	O
U	E	S	E	N	U	R	S
N	U	B	N	B	N	O	E
B	R	U	U	N	U	B	N
B	U	N	R	U	R	U	O
E	N	O	B	R	U	N	B

2 Pascale Michelon, 'Test your attentional focus: is multi-tasking a good thing?', Sharpbrains.com, 26 August 2010, https://sharpbrains.com/blog/2010/08/26/test-your-attentional-focus-is-multi-tasking-a-good-thing/

TEST 3

Try paying full attention to Tasks 1 and 2 given below:

423596286957467964786487652697 9

347647362453964739647893647835 2

173218848283482894672968725382 8

967287668286972369237679376826 2

169765882397929693226587677564 3

293647938648158862786864387356 9

Task 1: Count the number of times the number 9 appears above.

Task 2: Count the total number of times the numbers 2 and 8 appear in the above sequence.

You can judge your attention according to your score. The closer your score is to the right answer, the better attention you had while performing the test. This exercise helps you to test your attention on a particular task and also your attention span. Many people quit after the third or fourth line due to their short attention span. So if you were able to make it till the end, no matter what your score is, you have a good attention span. Moreover, this test involves our frontal lobe and parietal lobe, which deal with working memory, attention and visual interpretation among other things. These types of exercises are used in military training to improve attention span.

TEST 4

Count the number of times the letter F appears in the following sentence.

ONLY FEW PEOPLE

ARE AWARE OF THE

FACTS OF THE FAMOUS

LEANING TOWER OF PISA

How many did you find?

Solution

There are six F's in the above sentence but most people count only three. Why? We often don't correctly process the word 'OF'. We have probably read the word 'of' so many times in our life that we process it as one unit, overlooking the second letter/sound.

4

Train Your Mind, Change Your Brain

For nearly two hundred years, Western science believed that the mind, which is immaterial, cannot *influence* the brain, which is material. This belief was challenged in the early 1970s through the pioneering research of scientists like Michael Merzenich, Mriganka Sur, Richard Davidson, etc. The research conducted by Michael Merzenich showed that experience, coupled with attention, leads to physical changes in the structure and future functioning of the nervous system.[1] Attention, which is related to the mind, is capable of changing the structure of the brain. These experiments, and countless more since then have conclusively proven that the mind can impact the brain. Richard Davidson, of University of Wisconsin, Madison, has been researching Tibetan monks

---

[1] Sharon Begley, 'Mind over Matter,' in *Train Your Mind, Change Your Brain* (Ballantine Books, 2008) p. 159;.

M. M. Merzenich and R. C. deCharms, 'Neural Representations, Experience and Change,' in *The Mind-Brain Continuum*, ed. R. Llinás and P. S. Churchland (Boston: MIT Press, 1996), pp. 61–81.

for more than forty years to understand how a *trained mind* can *change the brain*.[2] Hence, the title of this chapter.

Consider this interesting experiment done by scientists in the 1970s[3]:

> Monkeys were fitted with headphones, and they were divided into two groups. Monkeys in the first group were trained to listen to the sounds from headphones while also getting their fingers tapped lightly. If they were able to perceive whenever the rhythm changed, they were rewarded with a sip of juice. The second group of monkeys (who were also listening to the sounds from headphones) were trained to pay attention not to the sounds from headphones, but to the change in rhythm of the taps on their fingers. After 6 weeks of this experimentation, the brain areas of both groups of monkeys were tested. Interestingly, auditory cortex (sound processing center of the brain) grew in size in the first group of monkeys (who were trained to notice changes in the sounds) and somatosensory cortex (touch processing center of the brain) grew in size in the second group of monkeys (who were trained to notice changes in the taps on their fingers).

[2] Richard Davidson, 'Brain Scans Show Meditation Changes Minds, Increases Attention,' 25 June 2007, Center for Healthy Minds, https://centerhealthyminds.org/news/brain-scans-show-meditation-changes-minds-increases-attention.

[3] Begley, *Train Your Mind*, 158;
    G. H. Recanzone, C. E. Schreiner and M. M. Merzenich, 'Plasticity in the Frequency Representation of Primary Auditory Cortex Following Discrimination Training in Adult Owl Monkeys,' *Journal of Neuroscience* 13 (1993): 87–103.

According to Helen Neville, the Canadian psychologist and neuroscientist of international renown, 'It's a beautiful experiment because it's showing the pure effect of attention. The stimulation was the same. The only thing that was different was what the monkeys were paying attention to. It's showing that attention is very necessary for neuroplasticity.'

While Merzenich said of the experiment, 'This leaves us with a clear physiological fact . . . moment by moment we choose and sculpt how our ever-changing minds will work, we choose who we will be the next moment in a very real sense, and these choices are left embossed in physical form on our material selves.'[4]

Neuroplasticity

As discussed in Chapter 2, we have truly learnt something new only when that information gets translated into a bunch of neural connections or networks inside the brain. This property of the brain to change its structure in response to our actions and thoughts is called *neuroplasticity*.

If you repeat a particular task again and again, this repetition strengthens the neural circuits corresponding to that activity. For example: if you are learning to play the guitar or any stringed instrument, the parts of the brain that process the stimuli from your fingers will grow neural connections. The stronger those connections, the easier it becomes to do that task. This is the result of neuroplasticity of the brain. This is how habits are formed.

---

[4] Begley, *Train Your Mind*, 159.

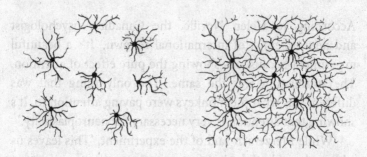

Neural connections before learning   Neural connections after learning

But the key is the role attention plays in this whole process. As you saw in the experiment with the monkeys—for neuroplasticity to work, you need to pay attention.

However, it is important to remember that neuroplasticity is value-neutral, i.e. the brain does not differentiate between which activity is repeated, as long as it is repeated with attention. If you allow your mobile to distract you repeatedly, then that is what becomes easier and easier for you to do. If you meditate every day, then that is what becomes easier and easier with each passing day.

Brain is a wonderful 'tathaastu' machine.
(wish-granting machine)

How your brain changes its shape and the kind of habits you develop depends on how and what you pay attention to. The brain provides the necessary biological infrastructure through neuroplasticity. How you harness its power is in your hands, because you are the master of your attention.

Until recently, it was believed that adult human brains could not grow new neurons. But now scientists have proven that human brains can grow new neurons all through their life.[5] These new neurons will migrate to those areas of the brain that are most active, i.e. the ones most engaged in learning. If these new neurons are not utilized or engaged, they die. This ability of the brain to grow new neurons is called *neurogenesis*.

It has been observed that

- new connections can grow with just a week's **practice**.[6]
- observable brain changes take place with just eight weeks' **practice**.
- new, positive habits can be created with **practice**.[7]

Practice is essentially the act of repeating an activity with focused attention.

Neuroplasticity and neurogenesis provide each of us the necessary biological factors required for our growth, provided we recognize their potential and steer our attention in the right direction.

As a student, when I [Aditi] used to prepare for exams, I could not tolerate any kind of disturbance. Even if someone was talking softly around me, it disturbed me a lot. As a result,

---

[5] S. Eriksson et al., 'Neurogenesis in the Adult Human Hippocampus', *Nature Medicine* 4 (1998): 1313–17.

[6] A. Pascual-Leone et al., 'Modulation of Muscle Responses Evoked by Trans-cranial Magnetic Stimulation during the Acquisition of New Fine Motor Skills', *Journal of Neurophysiology* 74 (1995): 1037–45.

[7] R.J. Davidson et al., 'Alterations in Brain and Immune Function Produced by Mindfulness Meditation', *Psychosomatic Medicine* 65, no.4 (2003): 564-70.

I studied in my room behind closed doors. My brain was conditioned to being easily disturbed.

What's most surprising is that years later, I attempted the national record of writing the table of a 13-digit-long number in the least time possible while sitting in a crowded restaurant with a noisy kitty party near me. I had gone to the restaurant for a meeting with the chief editor of *India Book of Records*. When I told him that I was practising for this particular record, he asked me to try it in front of him and I could do it in record time of 1 minute and 15 seconds. He was astonished to see me concentrate in such a chaotic place. When he asked me about it, I laughingly told him, 'This is all thanks to my children, who always make so much noise at home that I am used to practising in such conditions. Also, I practise meditation, which helps me hold my attention on one thing for long.'

Later, that record was made in even lesser time of 1 minute 13 seconds in the office of the Limca Book of Records.

When I first thought of attempting the record, I chose early mornings for my practice, as the rest of my family would be asleep then. I soon attained good speed. Then I started practising during the day, when my family members were following their regular routine. The phones and the doorbell would ring constantly, my kids would run around all the time, and the house help would be doing her chores all over the house. I would get distracted in the beginning, but slowly, with practice, I could hold my attention for longer periods of time. I commanded my mind to pay attention to my practice. Whenever other thoughts distracted me, I would say to my mind: 'Be here.' When I trained my mind like this and demanded attention and focus from it, my brain said, '*tathaastu*' (so be it), and with continued practice, I developed the *habit* of paying attention to my work, regardless of what was happening around me.

You too can train your mind to learn to pay attention for longer periods. Here are some exercises that you can practise to achieve that:

EXERCISES

1. ***Learn from the Spider***: When you hold a vibrating tuning fork next to a spider web, the spider comes to check what is shaking the web. But when you do it several times, the spider realizes that there is no bug or insect caught in its web and doesn't come looking for it again. Similarly, you can train yourself not to give in to distractions. Now practise this: when someone enters the room, or a car honks outside on the road, do not allow yourself to be distracted. Concentrate on what you were doing. This will take some time, but with practice you will get better and better.

2. ***Affirmations***: Keep your eyes open and look around while saying to yourself, 'I am good at concentration.' Repeat your affirmation with songs playing around you. If you start humming along, simply say 'No!' out loud and return to the affirmation with a little more intensity and exaggerated enunciation. Say it loudly, say it softly—do everything you can to make the affirmation so compelling that there's no room in your thoughts for anything else.

The goal is to keep your mind internally focused while your eyes and ears are outwardly focused. Continue practising until you can concentrate for at least five minutes even in an environment full of all kinds of distractions.

5

Attention as a Creator of Experience

The brain processes only those sensory stimuli that we pay attention to, which then become a part of our experience. Therefore, what we pay attention to every passing moment effectively decides how we experience those moments. Attention, coupled with our perspective, determines our state of mind at any given point of time.

A woman was busy running around the house, muttering to herself:

'I am fed up! So many bills to pay—gas, electricity, phone. On top of it, I have to cook for the relatives coming over today. This house is so big, it takes hours to clean it. How will I do it all? What kind of life is this?'

Complaining had become her habit. Cribbing about the traffic, pollution, inflation or even the house help's work was part of her daily routine. Just when she was clearing the dining table, her daughter's open notebook caught her attention. Her daughter had to write on the topic 'Turning Negatives to Positives' as part of her homework. She needed to jot down all the negative things in the course of her day and find something positive in them. Out of curiosity, the woman started reading what her daughter had written.

It read as follows:

- I had to take an awful medicine for a cold, but I am thankful, for it has made me feel better.
- I had a surprise test at school today and I did not perform well, but I am thankful because now I know the things I need to work on.
- I could not play badminton with my friends today as it was raining, but I loved making paper boats, which I had never done before.
- My mother gave me a peanut butter sandwich for packed lunch, which I hate, but I am happy to at least have something to eat, unlike so many other hungry kids in the world.
- I broke my smartphone today and had to use an old phone on which I couldn't even type, but I am happy I got to talk to my friends instead of just exchanging messages.

It then dawned on the mother that she had a lot of things to be thankful for as well! She thought again . . .

- I have so many bills to pay, but I am happy that I have access to so many facilities and the resources to pay for them.
- I had to make lunch for so many relatives, but I am thankful for having a family.
- It takes a lot of time to clean this big house, but I am happy that I have a roof over my head and such a beautiful house.

- My life is very hectic, but I am happy that it keeps me active and occupied.

Just as she reoriented her thoughts in such a manner, all her stress left her. She felt light and full of energy. She prepared the food with love, cleaned the house with excitement and paid all her bills calmly. Her day ended with expressing gratitude to God for the life she had.

> *What we decide to pay attention to and*
> *what we decide to ignore*
> *shapes our experiences and reality.*

If your focus is on negative things all around you, your experience will consist of negativity. But if your focus is on the positive things, your experience will be full of positivity. So, every moment that goes by, it is important to control our attention so that we start focusing on positive things.

In order to experience happiness, courage, confidence and peace in our lives, we need to learn to change the way we look at things; we need to change our perspective.

You can consider yourself a bag of weaknesses or of strengths. The perspective you choose determines the direction of your attention. If you consider yourself weak, then your attention will constantly be pulled towards your shortcomings and weaknesses, leading to unhappiness, anxiety, a sense of uncertainty and sorrow. But if you see yourself as strong, your attention will be redirected to your strengths and capabilities, resulting in you feeling more motivated, energetic and confident than before. This positive and focused state of mind will further increase the probability of you succeeding in any challenging task you then attempt. This mere change of perspective and shift in focus can completely transform the results you get on your efforts.

A lot of the sorrow that we experience is self-generated.

When our focus is external and we try controlling things that are not in our control, the inevitable result is disappointment and sorrow. When our focus is internal and we try controlling only the things that we can, and let go of those that we can't, the result is peace and happiness. From this perspective, attention creates our very state of mind and shapes our experience and our reality every single moment.

Stanford psychologist Carol Dweck echoes these thoughts—whichever aspects of a situation you pay attention to shapes your very mindset. When you experience failure, if your attention is on your feelings alone, then it would create a fixed mindset.[1] When you focus on feelings, you will try to avoid anything that is emotionally painful. And in this case, it's like avoiding the school exam instead of working on your lack of preparation for it. You will be inclined to associate the exam with so much sorrow.

Students often tend to think along these lines, 'Mathematics is difficult for me, so why not stop studying it? Why not take up other subjects that I'm already good at?' Because the feelings are unpleasant, they take up a large

---

[1]   K. Haimovitz and C. S. Dweck, 'What Predicts Children's Fixed and Growth Intelligence Mindsets? Not Their Parents' Views of Intelligence But Their Parents' Views of Failure,' *Psychological Science* (2016).

chunk of your attention, and continued focus on them turns them into sorrow. As human beings, we are always motivated to work towards minimizing our sorrows. If the task that you failed at brought you sorrow, you are not inclined to attempt it again to avoid the painful feelings of repeated failure. And soon, you develop a fixed mindset.

On the contrary, if you acknowledge—not dwell on— these difficult and sad feelings that arise from your failure and start focusing on the lessons learnt, you stay motivated and develop a growth mindset, and are then not afraid of failures. For example, if I failed in my mathematics exam, I will focus on the things I need to work on in order to succeed in my next attempt. This shift in perspective and hence focus, from hurt feelings to an opportunity to learn, is a sign of a growth mindset.

Whenever you are working from a position of strength, you will progress. But when you work from a position of weakness, your progress will be short-lived. It won't be sustainable or long-term. You should pick a strength, focus on it and then apply it. So, instead of saying, 'I should not get angry', you are going to say, 'let me be peaceful in the situation. What should I do in order to be peaceful in this situation?' This way, you are approaching from a position of strength and control, as you think of preparing yourself for a situation that is perhaps unavoidable. So your focus is not on your weakness (even though you are aware of it), but on your strength.

There is a difference between you being aware of your weakness and using it as the very foundation on which to base your efforts. You may be aware of your anger, but you are using your ability to stay calm as the foundation to bring about the change.

What is your ideal response to a particular situation? Pick a situation where you think you could do much better. What are the various strategies available for you to handle or respond to the situation in a better manner? Can you list them and start practising them?

For example, I can deliver my talks a lot better than I currently do. It is not that I am a weak speaker. But my focus is constantly on improvement, on adding value. My focus is not on feeling sad, mad and bad by thinking that I have a deficiency. I want to become one of the best speakers. So, what do I have to do to achieve that?

I have the following conversation with myself:

'I need to become calmer.'
'Okay. Practise that.'

'I need to remember the content of my speech.'
'Okay, then focus on going over the speech.'

'I need to be confident. I need to make eye contact with the audience.'
'Okay. Practise that. Use the visualization technique.'

On the contrary, if my focus is on what I want to avoid and everything that could go wrong, then I start thinking, 'I don't want to forget my speech. My hands and legs are shaking. I am a weak speaker,' and so on and so forth. The thing to remember is that the human mind is more easily attracted to weakness and negativity than positivity.[2] Even though negativity attracts you more, operating from a position of weakness is going to be detrimental for you.

In the above example, when you focus on '*not wanting to forget*', you are empowering your weakness of forgetting because that is what you are repeating. But instead, if you focus on '*wanting to remember*', then your ability to remember grows and you have automatically avoided forgetting.

When I focus on what I want to avoid, my mind is predominantly occupied with that. Inadvertently, by focusing on what I want to avoid, I am fuelling my weakness. In the short run, this focus on avoidance due to weakness might help, as the fear of loss can be a good motivator that will keep your actions measured and in check. But in the long run, avoidance due to the fear of loss will not help develop the necessary strength to overcome that weakness permanently.

That's why it is said that **fear is an excellent motivator, but a very bad navigator.**

So, it is always beneficial to develop a strength to replace a weakness, instead of just avoiding failures due to a weakness.

Learn to focus on your strengths and operate from a position of strength for sustainable progress.

---

2   Roy F. Baumeister et al., 'Bad Is Stronger Than Good,' *Review of General Psychology* 5 (2001), 323–370.

6

Spot the Virtues in Life

Wherever my attention goes, energy flows and
wherever my energy flows, life grows.

How can you make a line such as the one given below shorter without erasing or touching it?

———————————————

The answer is simple. By drawing a longer line below it.

————————————————————

Applying the same trick to life, we can make our weaknesses and vices seem smaller by working towards making our strengths and virtues bigger. But what about the weaknesses and vices of other people? How do you change people who are rude, mean, jealous, aggressive and do not have any positivity to share? It is not possible to work on their behaviours or weaknesses, is it? So how can we tackle their negative attributes?

Remember, focusing on things that are out of our control only brings us sorrow. But what you can control is focusing more on the positive attributes of people who are not nice to you. We can make their negatives seem small in comparison. The list of their weaknesses will automatically seem smaller when we make a list of their virtues. Initially you may find very few virtues in such a person, but eventually, when you start paying attention to their virtues, your experience with them will start becoming more positive.

I [Aditi] remember, a few years ago, a mother of a class seven student came to me with her son, worried about his recent loss of interest in mathematics. He had been doing very well in the subject till the previous year, but immediately after being promoted to the seventh grade, his interest and grades fell. After interacting with the child, I found that he was not very comfortable with his new teacher. I continued talking to him to learn about his other interests and hobbies, but inevitably the conversation would come back to his teacher, about whom he complained repeatedly. I found he was so obsessed with the negativity he perceived coming from the teacher that he was not able to focus on our conversation, and everything that I was offering to him was going to waste.

Then I asked him a simple question, *'Is it possible that there is not even a single good thing about her?'* He thought for a while and replied that she was very punctual. I asked him to think and write three good things about her and bring them to me the next day. A day later, he was very excited to share his homework with me, the three positive traits of his teacher. I suggested that he think only about these traits before her class. Within a few days, we noticed a change in his opinion about the teacher as well as with regard to the subject.

Life provides the cup, you choose what to fill it with.

Once, a professor gave his students a situation to consider while addressing them in class:

> 'You are holding a cup of coffee when someone comes along and bumps into you, or pats your arm, making you spill your coffee everywhere.'
>
> He asked them, 'Why do you think you spilt the coffee?'
>
> 'Because someone bumped into me!' one of the students said immediately.
>
> 'Wrong answer'.
>
> 'You spilt the coffee because there was coffee in your cup. Had there been tea in the cup, you would have spilt tea. Whatever is inside the cup is what will spill.'

Therefore, when life comes along and bumps into you or shakes you—which will happen—whatever is inside you will spill out. You feign calmness as the 'coffee' spills, but sooner or later, with repeated bumps, you will be rattled.

So, we have to ask ourselves, 'What's in my cup?' When life gets rough, *what* spills over from my cup? Joy, gratefulness, peace and humility? Or anger, bitterness, harsh words and knee-jerk reactions? Life provides the cup, *you* choose what to fill it with.

The human tendency is to see only other people's faults. And unknowingly, we fill our cup with these very shortcomings of other people, and that's what comes out when people rattle us and shake our cup—our negative reactions to all the negativity we collect.

When a friend doesn't return your call for a day, you think she doesn't care about you. When she calls up the next day, the thought that she doesn't care about you still runs through your mind. No matter what reason she gives you now, it will seem like a lame excuse because you have already filled your cup with a negative perspective about her. Instead, if you had been patient and thoughtful, considering the possibility that she could have been really busy to take your call, you would not have been so upset and would have listened to her now with concern.

Let us start working towards filling our cups with gratitude, forgiveness, joy, words of affirmation and kindness, gentleness and love and tolerance for others.

Spot the Virtue

To create a shift in your attitude towards other people, you need to inculcate the habit of spotting virtues in others. Here are some instructions on how to create a chart of your own that will help you spot and collect virtues, a chart that will be a depiction of a *rainbow of virtues.*

This is how you can prepare this chart:

- Draw a rainbow on a blank piece of paper.
- Choose seven qualities that, according to you, are most important.
- Assign each colour in the rainbow to one quality. For example, violet for honesty, indigo for helpfulness and so on.
- Pin this chart in your office workspace or your room, where you can see it every day.

Whenever you see anyone displaying any virtue mentioned in your rainbow, like being honest or helpful, mark a dot or paste a sticker in that colour for the respective quality on the chart.

Here is a list of qualities that can be put under 'Virtues' to get you started:

Acceptance, Accuracy, Attentiveness, Being Responsible, Benevolence, Cheerfulness, Cleanliness, Contentment, Cooperation, Courage, Determination, Discipline, Fearlessness, Flexibility, Generosity, Gentleness, Happiness, Honesty, Humility, Liberty, Lightheartedness, Love, Loyalty, Maturity, Mercy, Mental Stability, Obedience, Patience, Peacefulness, Perseverance, Respect, Self-confidence, Simplicity, Sweetness, Tirelessness, Tolerance, Trustworthiness, Unity, Wisdom

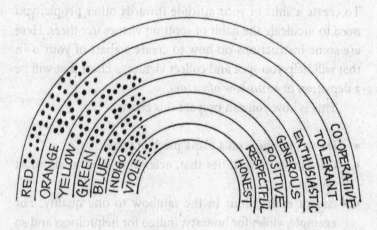

Practise this for at least twenty-one days and continue till your rainbow is filled up. Soon you will realize that it will turn into a habit, and you will see positive attributes in others without making an extra effort.

When you shift your attention to the positives around you, you feel motivated to imbibe these qualities in yourself too, thus becoming a better person. When we hear a friend donating for a cause, we may feel like contributing too. When we see someone picking up litter from the road, we may start looking for a bin to discard our trash. A dedicated sportsperson receiving an award inspires us to go after our dreams and work with renewed dedication.

Identifying virtues in others helps us to see the beauty in the world, in nature, in the small negligible things around us. It is then that we experience love and gratitude, and are in tune with God and the universe.

7

Unlock Your Talent

I [Aditi] often think about the time when I first went on stage
as a speaker to share the techniques of Vedic maths with an
audience of about 300 people! I still remember how difficult
it was to gather the courage to take the first step towards the
stage. In the beginning I felt a little nervous, but as I started,
the words flowed automatically, and my confidence grew
gradually. It became so natural, as if I was born to be on stage,
as if I had been waiting for this moment for a long time. That
was just the beginning and many more workshops followed,
each with an even larger audience than the previous. My
confidence kept growing with each experience.

In a conversation with my father, I once mentioned that
this was something beyond my imagination. As a timid and
shy child, I never thought that one day I would stand before
a huge audience and share my knowledge, experiences and
opinions without any hesitation. I marvelled at being able to
turn my biggest weakness into my biggest strength. My father
smiled and said, 'It's in your genes. Your grandfather was a
great motivator and a very impressive orator, even though he

wasn't very educated.' This made me think about my parents. Both of them are confident individuals who never hesitate to put forward their opinions among family and friends, in social settings or otherwise.

I wondered, if this was in my genes, why had I not expressed this trait for so many years? Why did I shudder at the very thought of going on stage, even to collect a prize?

After deep introspection, I found one answer to the above questions: **Wrong programming of the mind**. When I was a child, I used to see other people mesmerizing the audience with their speeches, and deep inside I wanted to be like them. But I believed they were born with this talent, and I was not. This self-doubt prevented me from taking up even a single chance to perform on stage, no matter how eager I was. So, with this wrong programming of my mind, I somehow ended up thwarting my natural talent and the genes that I had inherited from my grandfather and parents, who were all great at speaking in public. What I had done was locked my own genes away! And who knows, the people I saw speaking confidently on stage may not have had any natural propensity for the art of public speaking, but because they had the right programming in their mind, they worked towards getting better and *learnt* to become great public speakers!

HOW I UNLOCKED MY GENES

When I started gaining spiritual knowledge at a Brahma Kumaris centre, I learnt this:

We all are children of God and we have been given equal powers by the Almighty.

I started wondering, 'When God is my Father and I am His special child, why do I then feel nervous sharing my views in front of a small gathering? I asked one of the mentors at the centre, 'When others can do it, then why not me?'

She answered my question with a question. 'Can you find a single person in this world who is exactly like you?'

I said, 'No two people are exactly the same, not even identical twins. Then how can somebody be exactly like me?'

She said, '*This* is what you have to understand. Each one of us is unique and special in our own way. There cannot be any comparison. It is true that what somebody else can do, you may not do that exactly in the same way, but the way you can do a thing, nobody in this entire world can exactly match up to it. So, stop comparing yourself to others. **Discover your uniqueness, your strengths**.'

This made me search for my uniqueness and strengths. I found that I am good at sharing my experiences or learnings with others. I have always looked forward to sharing what I have learnt.

Those days I was learning Vedic maths techniques for my children, as I found these very interesting and useful for them. After teaching my own kids and looking at the positive results, I wanted to share these techniques with other children, so that they too could benefit. To fulfil this desire, I started taking classes in a small room in my house, for some children in my neighbourhood. Their surprised reactions and the excitement about learning these wonderful techniques filled me with a sense of achievement, for being able to make a positive difference in someone's life. This in turn gave a boost to my confidence to start sharing these learnings at bigger platforms. Soon, I got the opportunity to share my knowledge about Vedic maths techniques on stage, before a large audience, and this time, I did not let it pass. It had been my dream since childhood to go on stage with confidence. I felt the power of God giving me strength. With this new-found belief, I *unlocked my genes*, spoke confidently and realized my childhood dream.

You will be surprised to know that Sachin Tendulkar, one of the greatest cricket icons, who holds just about every batting record there is, actually wanted to become a fast bowler and not a batsman. In 1987, to fulfil his dream, he went to the MRF Pace Foundation in Chennai, run by Australian fast bowler Dennis Lillee. Lillee wasn't impressed by his bowling. He saw him during batting practice in the nets and told him to stick to batting and forget about bowling. Sachin was adamant on becoming a bowler, but Lillee insisted that he should focus on batting. Lillee must have noticed that Sachin's natural talent lay in batting.

And what advice it turned out to be! It gave us the man who would go on to be known as the 'God of Indian cricket'.

So, what is *your* natural talent? Ask yourself these three simple questions:

- **What is it that you are passionate about?**
- **Do you enjoy doing it even if you are very tired?**
- **Do you think you will be able to excel at it with little effort?**

Now, try to think how you can use your talent for the betterment of society so that it gets meaning and purpose. Work to polish your innate talent till you shine at it.

MASTERING THE SKILLS NOT IN YOU

But what if you want to do something that is not your natural talent?

Is it possible to concentrate on and master those skills as well?

From my own learnings and accounts of other successful people, I can say it surely is. Even if you don't have any particular talent, you can work on developing one and create the required connections in your brain!

You might be surprised to hear this from the person who has penned five books, but writing was not my forte. A lot of teachers and students who attended our workshops on Vedic maths and memory insisted that Sudhir and I write a book on these wonderful techniques. They reasoned that it would help these techniques reach and benefit a large number of people who might miss out on this knowledge otherwise. I wasn't too thrilled with the idea, as I used to find it difficult to write even a simple email and preferred instead to speak on the phone. But I thought of giving it a try and started reading various books to get an idea on how to go about it. The more I read, the more I felt discouraged, as I thought I would not be able to present my knowledge and my narrative the way the other books had. My husband, Sudhir, advised me not to be discouraged or intimidated by works of other people. He reminded me that I am unique, and so is my way of writing. He believed the simplicity of my writing would be its biggest strength. Trusting his words, I started writing but found it really difficult to keep going. When he saw my lack of motivation, he showed me a bigger picture, a bigger purpose. He pushed me to see how our book would serve millions of students across the world who are waiting to learn these techniques and will benefit from it. His encouragement gave me the drive to work relentlessly without giving up, as now I had a clear vision of what my efforts were directed at.

Within a few months, we released our first book, *How to Become a Human Calculator*.[1] The book became a bestseller in no time, and today we are on to our sixth book as I write this. I say with pride that all our books are doing well.

Giving my mind a meaningful purpose and working hard with strong self-belief helped me concentrate to develop a skill that was not my natural talent. In fact, it was something that I always wanted to escape from.

Clarity of vision and the ultimate purpose of a task makes one more interested and invested in completing it. The clearer the end result, the better your concentration on your task.

To find a purpose in your task, ask yourself these questions:

- **How will this task change my life?**
- **How is it going to impact others' lives?**
- **How is it going to impact society in a positive way?**

---

[1] Aditi Singhal and Sudhir Singhal, *How to Become a Human Calculator*, (Delhi: S. Chand and Co., 2012).

8

Attention Enhancers

Today's economy is no longer the *information economy*, but rather the *attention economy*. What everyone is looking for is a piece of your attention. Whichever 'free' social media platform you use—Facebook, Twitter, LinkedIn, Youtube, etc.—is not actually free. You are 'paying' in the form of your attention, which is the most important human as well as economic resource. When you use Google, Facebook, Twitter, Youtube, etc., your personal data is being used by these companies to make money through targeted advertising. You are spending your most important resource, your attention, without being mindful about it, and mistakenly believing the service you're using is free!

There is no such thing as a truly free online service in this world.

In this attention economy, if you want to excel and make unique contributions in your field, you must not only learn to safeguard your attention, you must also learn to enhance it.

If you follow the herd, doing what others are doing, you will never be recognized. But if you want to be recognized and become the best at something, learn to focus on protecting your attention. Use that process to invest your energy in creating something unique and challenging. Because playing games on a phone or a tablet, surfing the Web and watching online videos is something even a three-year-old child can do today. What about doing something different? Only then will you grow and be recognized in today's world.

Our busy lifestyle and daily routine affect our ability a great deal to pay complete attention to our required tasks. How we decide to spend our time and what we choose to take in and what we choose to block out from our attention is very important and must be consciously decided by us every moment. Even the few minutes of our free time, if well spent, can empower us to decide where we should invest our attention. A healthy body, along with a positive and healthy mind, is a prerequisite as well as a vital tool for enhancing our attention.

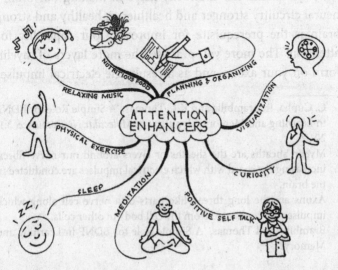

Here are some important attention enhancers for your benefit.

1. PHYSICAL EXERCISE

As you read in Chapter 4, the brain physically changes its structure when we learn something new. We can say we learnt something when the corresponding neural circuits form inside the brain to 'capture' this new information. Research shows that the ability of neurons to connect with each other and transmit electrical signals among themselves is key when it comes to the formation of these neural circuits[1]. These electrical impulses (ones that are formed when learning something new) travel faster and more accurately in proportion to the strength of myelin sheath[2] that cover the axons[3] of these neurons.

Brain Derived Neurotropic Factor (BDNF) has been found to help increase the strength of myelin. BDNF is produced by the brain when you perform physical exercise.[4] So, physical exercise indirectly helps in making our brain's neural circuitry stronger and healthier. A healthy and strong brain is the prerequisite for improving our capability for attention. The more you practise, the more layers of myelin form on your axons, and as a result, the electrical impulses

---

[1] C. Cunha, R. Brambilla and K.L. Thomas, 'A Simple Role for BDNF in Learning and Memory?' *Frontiers in Molecular Neuroscience*, 3:1, 2010.

[2] Myelin sheaths are the sheaths or layers around our nerve fibres, increasing the speed with which electrical impulses are conducted in the brain.

[3] Axons are the long thread-like parts of a nerve cell along which impulses are conducted from the cell body to other cells.

[4] Brambilla and Thomas, 'A Simple Role for BDNF in Learning and Memory?'

travel along the axons' more quickly and accurately, and finally your brain acquires more 'skill'. In short, BDNF helps in the development of a better, stronger and healthier brain. This helps in improving your attention.[5]

Exercise may not just increase the amount of learning but also your *rate* of learning, i.e., you will learn things faster when you exercise. As many of us might have experienced, **exercise also reduces anxiety and stress**, as well as the risk of heart attack, diabetes and high BP. It strengthens the bones, muscles and joints, and improves the immune system, but most importantly, it is an **effective happiness booster**.

Even if you exercise for fifteen to twenty minutes a day, it's a very good start.

2. NUTRITIOUS FOOD

You would have noticed that when your mind is disturbed, or your body is weak, you are not able to focus or pay attention for long periods of time. So, a healthy body and a healthy brain are prerequisites for long attention spans. Anything that improves your physical health and brain health improves your ability to pay attention and focus on the task at hand.

'Annamayam hi soumya manah'
(Your mind is filled with the food that you eat)

---

[5]   E.M. Galloway, N.H. Woo and Bai Lu, 'Persistent Neural Activity in the Prefrontal Cortex: a Mechanism by which BDNF Regulates Working Memory?' *Progress in Brain Research* 169: no. 251 (2008).

The above quote is from the Chandogya Upanishad. It means whatever you eat impacts your thinking, that is, *as is the food, so is the mind*.

The brain weighs about 2 per cent of body weight, but accounts for 20 per cent of the total energy used by the body. Nutritious food is very important for a healthy brain. Research in the new field of nutritional psychiatry shows the impact of food on the brain and on mental health.

Dr Felice Jacka, director of Food and Mood Center, Deakin University, Australia, and a pioneer in the field of nutritional psychiatry, correctly said, *'Food is something that is prepared in a kitchen. Food is not something that is manufactured in a factory by a chemist.'* Some insights from Dr Jacka's latest book, *Brain Changer*, can be useful here:[6]

- Food high in sugar, salt and additives increases the probability of anxiety and depression.
- Processed or *interfered food* is bad for health.
- While processed food can provide calories, it provides little or no nutrients, which are vital for body's health. This leads to malnutritive obesity.
- Food consumed by the mother and the father during conception and pregnancy can impact the mental health of the newborn.
- Traditional food that incorporates vegetables, fruits, nuts, whole grains, is far superior to processed junk food.

---

[6] Felice Jacka, *Brain Changer* (Yellow Kite, 2019).

India and Nutrition

The number of cases of obesity and people being overweight has tripled since 1990. That's the year Coca-Cola and Pepsi were set up in India. Since 2010, the sale of packaged food has increased 140 per cent and the sale of junk food by more than 80 per cent.[7]

If the current trend of consumption of junk or processed food continues in India, by 2040, the number of people diagnosed with type-2 diabetes will increase to 12 crores in our country. Eating junk food, which is not nutritious, adversely impacts our brain and body. When you add chemicals to naturally occurring foods, you are interfering with their natural capability, and that 'interfered food' is bad for physical and mental health, and thus also bad for your ability to be attentive.

3. SLEEP

Sleep has a profound impact on our ability to focus and perform efficiently and effectively.[8] Improper or insufficient sleep is one of the major contributors to many of the mental and physical health problems in today's sleep-deprived world. Our own subjective experience shows that even one night's sleep deprivation can make us groggy, increase our irritation levels and decrease our attention span.

---

[7] John Read, *From Alchemy to Chemistry*, (New York: Dover Publications, 2011), pp. 179–180.

[8] L. Kirszenblat and B. van Swinderen, 'The Yin and Yang of Sleep and Attention,' *Trends in Neurosciences* 38, no.12 (2015): 776–786.

Sleep deprivation or lack of sufficient sleep has been shown to have an adverse impact on alertness levels and on concentration. Total sleep deprivation not only impairs attention and working memory, but it also affects other functions, such as long-term memory and decision-making. Partial sleep deprivation is found to influence attention, especially vigilance.[9]

Here are some important things to remember the next time you want to stay up late on a weeknight and know you won't be able to get as much sleep as you need.

- **Sleep enriches our ability to learn and memorize by improving our attention.** Research shows that if you want to learn, memorize and remember any important concepts, always ensure you get a good night's sleep.[10] Because when you sleep well, the information in your memory gets transferred to the hippocampus[11] and starts functioning as long-term memory. If you are sleep-deprived, this does not happen properly.

---

[9] P. Alhola and P. Polo-Kantola, 'Sleep deprivation: Impact on Cognitive Performance', *Neuropsychiatric Disease and Treatment 3*, no. 5 (2007): 553–567.

[10] Matthew Walker, 'Too Extreme for the Guiness Book of World Records: Sleep Deprivation and the Brain' in *Why we Sleep*, Scribner, 2017: pp. 133-163;

J. Lim and D.F. Dinges, 'Sleep Deprivation and Vigilant Attention. Molecular and Biophysical Mechanisms of Arousal, Alertness, and Attention' *Annals of the New York Academy of Science* 1129, (2008) 305-322.

[11] Located in the inner temporal lobe, the hippocampus is the centre of memory in the brain.

- **Sleep improves your psychological health**, because when you have a good night's sleep, your ability to withstand psychological stress increases. Therefore, sleep functions as a *psychological shock absorber*.
- **Sleep inspires creativity through dreams**. August Kekulé, the famous chemist who discovered the circular structure for benzene got this insight from his dream.[12]
- **Sleep fine-tunes the balance of insulin and circulating glucose.** One of the most significant aspects of your health is to keep your glucose levels within a healthy range. This is because when you don't sleep properly, the fine balance between the insulin and the circulating glucose goes haywire and can lead to poor absorption of glucose. This can increase the probability of insulin resistance and lead to type-2 diabetes.
- **Sleep impacts our metabolism, and the cardiovascular, immune and reproductive systems.**

Sleep Hygiene Tips

- *Do not use your mobile phone at least for an hour before your sleep time.*
- *Do not exercise too late in the evening,* because you are not supposed to stimulate your body and therefore the brain before you sleep. It will take you that much longer to fall asleep if you exercise. Do not exercise at least two hours prior to your bedtime.
- *Avoid large meals and beverages late at night.* Don't indulge in rich foods like biryani and noodles; don't

---

[12] Read, *From Alchemy to Chemistry*, pp. 179–180.

have midnight snacks and definitely avoid coffee late at night.

- *Having the right sunlight exposure during the daytime* also helps you sleep well at night.

4. POSITIVE SELF-TALK

The way you talk to yourself about a situation internally greatly affects the way you cope with it externally. Every situation has two components, the *facts* in the situation and the *story* you tell yourself about those facts. Self-talk is that story, the steady stream of thoughts or internal dialogue that goes on in our minds constantly.

Negative self-talk can diminish confidence, lead to a lot of anxiety and stress, and also failure. Prolonged negative self-talk can also lead to hopelessness and depression. In contrast, when we speak positively to ourselves, it enhances our attention, improves our ability to focus on the task at hand, improves our efficiency and effectiveness, helps control our emotional reactions and, most importantly, helps manage our stress.

Negative self-talk activates the emotional centres of our brain and, in extreme cases, completely switches off our thinking or rational brain. Positive self-talk shifts the control from our emotional brain to our thinking brain and helps improve attention.

DEFAULT NEGATIVE SELF-TALK	CONSCIOUS POSITIVE SELF-TALK
Oh my God, it's the same question again! I got it wrong last time. I am sure I will get it wrong again.	Just because I got it wrong last time does not mean it will happen again. Let me try once again.
I would rather avoid this opportunity than risk failure and rejection.	If I fail or get rejected, I will still accept myself and learn from my experiences to do better next time.
Someone or something is making me feel utterly miserable and depressed.	No one and nothing can make me feel depressed. I control my emotions.
I cannot forget my past experiences. My feelings or behaviour today will continue to be strongly affected by it.	The past only affects the present for as long as I allow myself to not get healed by the traumatic past events. I have a choice here.
I can't talk in public. I'll forget everything . . . I've always stumbled over my words when it really mattered. Last time I was so nervous I sounded like a robot . . .	I can handle this. I just need to relax and take a deep breath. I have rehearsed this. I am prepared.

By becoming aware of the *story* you tell yourself, you can consciously transform the negative self-talk into positive self-talk. Positive self-talk, even during trying circumstances, has the potential to relax the self and increase attention by strengthening the executive circuits of the brain.

Before you start any difficult task, it is very important that you set aside a few minutes to become aware of your self-talk and consciously transform it into positive. Some examples are given in the table above. This little bit of positive pep talk can dramatically improve your performance at any task. Positive self-talk before the start of a race has been shown to improve the attention and performance of even athletes.

Next time you are about to start doing a task or give any performance, try motivating yourself to improve your attention.

5. LISTENING TO RELAXING MUSIC

Music has been shown to relax the mind of the listener and help reduce mental 'chatter'. This reduction in the chaos in the mind increases the focus and thus improves attention. When you listen to your preferred music, both your mind and body relax by activating the parasympathetic nervous system, which in turn invokes the body's *rest and digest* response (opposite of the *fight or flight* response caused by stress). And *a calm mind is a prerequisite for concentration.*

A relaxed mind invokes relaxation response and relaxation response[13] has been shown to increase focus by strengthening the executive functions of the brain.

According to a research, music students (learning either instrumental or vocal) who listened to their preferred genres were able to focus better and complete more tasks correctly,

---

[13] P.M. Scheufele, 'Effects of Progressive Relaxation and Classical Music on Measurements of Attention, Relaxation, and Stress Responses', *Journal of Behavioral Medicine* 23, (2000): 207–228.

as compared to those who were not studying music.[14] This goes on to show how appreciation of music can enhance your attention and focus.

6. CURIOSITY

Curiosity puts the brain in a learning state. The motivation to learn increases when you are curious. In a curious state of mind, one asks probing questions. And a question has the power to temporarily shut off unnecessary thoughts and increase focus.

Curiosity is asking a series of questions to understand any task or phenomenon. And asking questions and taking interest improves attention.

For example: Just inviting employees to ask 'What if . . .?' and 'How might we . . .?' questions about their organization's goals and plans can have a big impact.

What if we start giving our product for free and still make money?

How is WhatsApp making money?

Asking questions means there is a desire to understand things better. Attention and thinking are not driven by answers. They are driven by questions. This has been covered in more detail in Chapter 11, 'Asking the Right Questions'.

---

[14] A. Darrow, C. Johnson, S. Agnew, E. Fuller and M. Uchisaka, 'Effect of Preferred Music as a Distraction on Music Majors and Nonmusic Majors' Selective Attention', *Bulletin of the Council for Research in Music Education* 170, (2006): 21-31.

7. PLANNING AND ORGANIZING

When our surroundings are chaotic, it becomes difficult for us to focus. For example, if you have to find your pen amid the disorganized mess on your desk, it will take you longer and may lead to frustration and, in extreme cases, to anxiety.

But when things are organized, it takes very little mental and physical energy to find something we need or to work in that space with a focused mind. When you sit to study or do some important work, make sure that all necessary things, such as reference material, notebooks, stationery, files, hard drives, etc., are handy and within reach, so that you don't have to get up again and again to fetch one thing or the other. Keep all these things in an organized manner so as not to create clutter.

This reduction in *psychic entropy* (disturbance in the mind) also enhances our attention. Before you start any task, it is very important that you ask simple questions, like What, Why, How, Where, With Whom, When, etc. Once you achieve this clarity, it becomes easier to focus. Clarity—both external and internal—calms an anxious mind, and a *clear mind is a wellspring of concentration.* The more planned and organized you are, the easier it becomes to pay attention. Planning and organizing remove the unnecessary clutter, both in our surroundings and in our minds, and help improve our focus.

Clarity in Goals

Just like you need physical and mental clarity for better attention, a clearly defined goal goes a long way to increase your chances of attaining it. Only when you *see* your destination can you plan a road map that will lead you to it.

Clearly show your mind what has to be achieved in the given time. Create a road map in your mind to reach the goal. Our final destination may be far, but when we mark various milestones on the way, it makes our journey less challenging, as we know already how we are going to get there.

Similarly, a goal may seem too overwhelming as a whole. But when it is broken into smaller goals, it does not seem that difficult. Let's say you are studying for your Class 12 exams. Your dream is to get into the best college for design in your town or city after that. How are you going to break it down into smaller goals?

- The first goal should be to achieve distinction in your class.
- The second goal can be to shortlist the colleges.
- The third goal should be to pass the entrance exams for the respective colleges.
- Then to get through the interviews.

All these goals require different kinds of preparations.

Each of the above goals can be further split into smaller goals or milestones. With the passing of each of these milestones, your confidence will increase. Prepare daily, weekly and monthly targets and evaluate your performance at each step. It is also important to reward yourself after each small or big success.

This whole process of setting a goal and achieving intermediate milestones is just like playing a video game. While playing, we have continuous visual goals to achieve, which keep our brain active and stimulated throughout. As we begin to complete level after level, it leads to dopamine rush,[15] which then gives us a feeling of accomplishment and happiness. This serves as a motivating factor to continue our efforts and achieve new targets. Similarly, achieving each milestone, no matter how small, will motivate you to move closer towards your chosen goal.

8. VISUALIZATION

Fear, anxiety and uncertainty are the worst enemies of attention. Anything done to minimize these three will automatically improve our attention. Visualization is one such technique that has been proven to help improve attention and focus, even during trying times. Visualization means *creating a picture in the mind.* Your brain cannot distinguish between imagining something and actually experiencing it. It is this property of the brain that can be harnessed to improve the focus and attention by *visualizing* certainty, by visualizing success and thus reducing the fear, anxiety and uncertainty in any situation.

Let's illustrate this with an example: Imagine you are going to make your first sales presentation to a prospective customer. You are very anxious and are not able to focus. Now, try visualizing yourself successfully delivering the presentation and practise it enough times in your mind. You will notice your anxiety reducing, because you were able to see yourself successfully delivering the presentation. Since the brain cannot distinguish reality from imagination, it starts responding to your visualization as if you have already succeeded. This feeling of success removes the uncertainty temporarily from your

---

[15] Dopamine rush is explained in detail in Chapter 15, 'Digital Wellness', page 142.

mind and reduces your anxiety, which in turn increases your focus when you actually deliver your presentation.

Your 'experience' of success in any task, using visualization, is directly proportional to the extent of detail to which you can visualize. Here is an example of detailed visualization for the above example: You are standing in the room before your clients, wearing your favourite clothes; each of your clients is sitting in a specific order; all of them are nodding their heads in agreement as you speak, you see them applauding and congratulating you at the end of the presentation, and so on.

Neuroscientists have discovered that visualization establishes neural pathways in the brain that act as a blueprint to be followed in the actual performance.[16]

That is to say, when you visualize successfully delivering the presentation, the neural circuits corresponding to the delivery of the presentation start forming inside your brain. These neural circuits serve as blueprint when you actually deliver the presentation, as if you have practised it many times before your clients. Because you are familiar with your clients, the room and the overall scene of you delivering the presentation, your brain is no longer reactive or anxious. *Familiarity reduces anxiety and improves focus.*

---

[16] A. Pascual-Leone, D. Nguyet, L.G. Cohen, J.P. Brasil-Neto, A. Cammarota, M. Hallett, 'Modulation of Muscle Responses Evoked by Transcranial Magnetic Stimulation during the Acquisition of New Fine Motor Skills', *Journal of Neurophysiology* 74, no. 3 (1995):1037-45;
M. Bangert, E.O. Altenmüller, 'Mapping Perception to Action in Piano Practice: a Longitudinal DC-EEG Study'. *BMC Neuroscience* 4, no. 26 (2003).

It is not just for working professionals but for people from all walks of life. Let's assume, you are preparing for a dance competition. Visualize yourself dancing confidently on stage, following all your steps to a T. Hear people applauding you. Feel your emotions. How happy you are to give the best performance of your life! Think about how proud your parents, mentors and friends are of your achievement. When you clearly see the fruits of your labour, you feel motivated to march ahead. Never let the thought of failure cross your mind. Visualization helps increase familiarity with the stressful situation you are about to face and thus helps improve your focus and attention.

Visualization is also a great memory-enhancing tool. It can help you convert boring text into interesting images or movies, so that you can retain it in your mind for a longer period of time. This is because our mind understands the language of images. Let's look at an example. Suppose you are reading about Gandhi's role in the freedom struggle. Try to visualize the text while you are reading. Imagine yourself accompanying Gandhi. Imagine he is sharing his feelings about the British with you and his plan of action to confront them. That way, you will get emotionally involved in the scene and will feel like you're a part of a movie and it's actually happening with you. As mentioned earlier, your brain cannot distinguish between your imaginings and your real experiences. And we tend to remember our experiences for a much longer time.

To know more about visualization and memory techniques, refer to our earlier book *How to Memorize Anything*.[17]

---

[17] Aditi Singhal and Sudhir Singhal, *How to Memorize Anything* (Penguin Random House India, 2015).

9. MEDITATION AS ATTENTION TRAINING

Meditation empowers and recharges the mind by channelizing our thoughts in the right direction while enabling us to keep in touch with our higher consciousness. The process of meditation not only helps the mind to relax by reducing the number of thoughts but also leads to attitudinal change by cleansing all negative and wasteful thoughts. It helps in consciously creating positive thoughts about the self and others, thereby elevating the quality of thoughts.

Rather than becoming anxious and worrying about controlling everything in our complex world, with meditation we can gain control over the things that *can* be brought under our control. That redirection is what increases our focus, because we are no longer wasting our energy and time in trying to control things that cannot be controlled.

Research shows that meditation helps reducing activity in the amygdala, the emotional centre of our brain, thus reducing and regulating our anxiety and emotional reactions.[18] It also helps strengthen the prefrontal cortex, which is also called the rational or thinking brain, thus increasing our focus. The more you practise meditation, the stronger the neural circuits corresponding to your emotional regulation become, thanks to neuroplasticity that we discussed in Chapter 4.

Negative rumination removes our focus from our work and increases our anxiety and fear. Meditation, which involves heightened awareness of the present moment,

---

[18] R.J. Davidson, J. Kabat-Zinn, et al., 'Alterations in brain and immune function produced by mindfulness meditation', *Psychosomatic Medicine* 65 (2003), 564-570.

involves attending to your thoughts *intentionally* and *non-judgementally*. It helps reduce negative rumination and promotes positive self-reflection, which in turn reduces anxiety and improves focus. Positive self-talk and meditation strengthen the prefrontal cortex and improve the executive functioning of the brain, and thus help increase focus and attention.

How to Meditate?

There are different types of meditation. But here we would like to share the technique of Raja Yoga meditation, which we [Aditi, Sudhir and Bala] have been practising for many years. We have experienced profound positive changes in our ways of thinking, and in our beliefs and perceptions, our ways of seeing others and our work efficiency. In Raja Yoga meditation, we particularly aim to: **Think Less, Think Slow and Think Better.**

For that, we constantly try to keep a check on our thoughts, which precede the words we speak and actions we perform. So, paying attention to the self at the thought level, where a lot of chaos originates very subtly, is an important step in meditation. By keeping a constant check on our minds, we consciously choose to dispel our negative, wasteful thoughts, and create positive, empowering thoughts, thereby changing our feelings and experiences in any given situation.

In simple words, meditation can be described as a three-step process: *Check, Choose* and *Change*.

Let's say a student is feeling very nervous before his final match in a badminton championship. All sorts of negative and fearful thoughts cloud his mind:

I have just recovered from an injury.
The opponent is very strong.
I always make silly errors in the game.
What if I make mistakes this time too?
What if I am not able to beat him?
What if I get injured again?

Such thoughts will make him feel weak and take away his confidence. What he can do here is: **check** these thoughts by observing them; **choose** to create positive, empowering thoughts about his performance; and **change** his feelings and experience about the whole situation. Thoughts he may consciously choose to create can be:

I am a good badminton player.
I am unique in my own way and can think creatively.
I know I can do it.
I am getting better day by day. I have done a great deal of practice.
I am feeling confident about my performance.
I am a special child of the almighty God and He is there to help and guide me.
I am receiving God's powers and blessings.

By creating such positive thoughts, we shift our attention from feeling nervous to feeling empowered, more confident and focused.

In meditation, we not only create positive thoughts in mind but also visualize them using our intellect and try to be in that state of mind, experiencing the positive visualizations.

Thus, our **mental and intellectual faculties work together, yielding better concentration**.

Meditation Practice

Sit in a comfortable position with your back straight. You can either sit on a cushion on the floor cross-legged or, if this is uncomfortable, sit on a chair. Choose a quiet place away from noise and visual distraction. Gentle background music can be played, as this helps to create a relaxed atmosphere. If you wish, you could position this book in front of you and read the following words slowly and silently. Aim to experience and visualize the words in your mind so that you begin to feel what is being described.

Thoughts for Meditating

Nothing exists outside this room . . .

I am feeling completely isolated from the outside world and free to explore my inner world . . .

I am turning all my attention inwards, concentrating my thoughts and energies on the centre of my forehead . . .

I am becoming aware of the stillness around me and within me . . .

A feeling of natural peacefulness is beginning to spread over me . . .

Waves of peace are gently washing over me, removing any restlessness and tension from my mind . . .

I am concentrating on this feeling of deep peace . . .

Just peace . . .

I . . . am . . . peace . . .

Peace is my true state of being . . .

My mind is becoming very calm and clear . . .

I am feeling relaxed and content . . . having returned to my natural consciousness of peace . . .

I shall sit for a while, enjoying this feeling of calmness and serenity . . .

Practise repeating this or similar thoughts to yourself for about ten minutes, at least two times a day.

You may use the following link to listen to guided meditation commentaries and experience it:

http://www.aditisinghal/meditation

We have presented nine attention enhancers in this chapter. We encourage you to explore and experiment with them, and experience for yourself which set of enhancers works best for you. Some of these are easy (like listening to relaxing music), and some of these require changes in your lifestyle (eating nutritious food, avoiding junk food and adopting healthy sleeping habits). But all of these will enhance your attention and your ability to focus significantly. Why not try as many as you can and see for yourself?

9

9

Why Do We Get Distracted?

At 10 o'clock on Monday morning, Sumit sat with his laptop to work on a very important office project. He needed to write a proposal for a new client he was pitching to in two days. But three phone calls, ten emails, two trips to the bathroom and five impromptu conversations with his colleagues later, the main task was still pending. In the middle of it all, he had spent thirty minutes booking a family vacation, and now his assistant had reminded him of a lunch meeting that was due in fifteen minutes.

Aryan had a routine office meeting that he was least interested in attending. But now that he was in it and bored, he casually pulled out his phone and began to go through his emails. He was completely absorbed in his handheld device when he suddenly heard Rishi, his boss, call out his name. Aryan looked up as Rishi asked, 'Aryan, what do you think we should do?' Aryan had no idea what Rishi was referring to.

Sumit had planned to write his proposal, but a number of other tasks pushed him off his path. Although those tasks were important, at the end of the day, his proposal remained unwritten.

Aryan certainly had not intended to completely lose himself in his gadget; the emails weren't even that important. But his distraction quickly became his focus and, during that moment, when his opinion was critical, all he could do was look up at his boss with a blank expression.

Living the life we want requires not only doing the right things but also steering away from the wrong ones that take us off the track.

Any object, person or thought, i.e., any kind of stimulus that diverts our attention from where it's supposed to be is a *distraction*.

A TIMELESS CHALLENGE

Our world has always been full of things designed to distract us. Today, we put all the blame on technology, but not giving in to distractions has been a challenge for ages. A few decades ago, people complained about the brain-numbing power of the television. Before that, it was the radio, the landline telephone, magazines and comic books. Though most of these things seem dull and boring in comparison to today's enticements, it is a fact of life that there have been and always will be things to distract us and weaken our focus.

Today's distractions, however, are different in nature. The endless assault of unending data and information, streaming through to us at superfast speed, with the ever-present access to new content on our handheld devices, means the world can be way more distracting than it ever was. Accessibility and affordability have increased and so have the reasons due to which we give in to distractions. If it's a distraction you seek, it is easier than ever to find it!

Earlier, there used to be fewer interruptions like these. People had to physically come to you to speak because they didn't have pagers, cell phones or the Internet.

'People think focus means saying yes to the thing you have got to focus on. But that is not what it means at all. It means saying no to the hundred other good ideas that there are. You have to pick carefully'—Steve Jobs

A RESEARCH ON DISTRACTION TIME:

A study conducted by Gloria Mark, of the University of California, found that it takes an average of **23 minutes and 15 seconds to refocus on a task after an interruption,** i.e. distractions derail your mental thought process for about half an hour. In other words, interrupting your work to check a message on your phone doesn't just take 30 seconds, but 23 minutes and 15 seconds, as it will take that much more time for you to regain the same focus. Just imagine the work that you are doing being repeatedly getting pushed back throughout the day. On an average, people switch tasks and self-interrupt themselves every **3 minutes and 5 seconds.**[1]

$$\begin{array}{c} \text{Duration of} \\ \text{distraction} \end{array} + \begin{array}{c} \text{23 minutes} \\ \text{15 seconds} \end{array} = \begin{array}{c} \text{Actual duration} \\ \text{of distraction} \end{array}$$

---

[1] Kermit Pattison, 'Worker, Interrupted: The Cost of Task Switching', FastCompany.com, 7 July 2008, https://www.fastcompany.com/944128/worker-interrupted-cost-task-switching

WHAT LEADS TO DISTRACTION

In one of our workshops, a participant shared his experience. He had switched to an old keypad cellphone from his smartphone, without any Internet connectivity on it, so that he would not be tempted to use WhatsApp, Instagram and Facebook, which used to take away all his attention. But then he found it difficult to get around without GPS and the quick and easy access to his emails. He missed listening to motivational podcasts on his smartphone while travelling as well.

To reduce his time online, he subscribed to the print edition of the newspaper that he used to read online. But after a few days, he ended up with a stack of unopened newspapers, as he found himself hooked to the news on TV instead. To avoid that distraction, he started working in an e-free room, that is, a room with no gadgets or Internet connectivity. However, whenever he would sit down to write, he would find himself attracted to the bookshelf in front of him. He would pick up a book with the intention of spending only a few minutes reading it, which would eventually turn into hours!

All of this just goes on to show that the real source of his problem was not the *availability* of distractions around him (smartphones, keypad phones, newspapers, TV, books) from which he kept running, but his habit of *getting distracted* by them. So, he just kept on replacing one distraction with another, without achieving the focus he wanted.

People believe that with emerging digital technology, mobiles and other gadgets are becoming the major source of distraction, which in one way is true. But technology has its advantages as well. We need to develop the wisdom and mental strength to use technology wisely, and to our advantage.

We will discuss in detail how to make the right use of technology while dealing with digital distractions in Chapter 15, 'Digital Wellness'. But before we go there, let's talk about *the four major factors that lead to a distracted mind.*

1. Boredom

Children feel bored after studying even for a few minutes but enjoy a three-hour-long movie as they are able to connect with it emotionally. Our mind connects to things and situations where we are able to feel emotions. In a class, the student who can emotionally visualize his success by listening to the lecture will be able to concentrate better than the rest of the students. So, it's very important to connect with the work at hand emotionally, because only then we will find it interesting. When we feel bored, we look for some stimulation, something from where we can get immediate pleasure or instant gratification. It can be something external, like reaching out for our mobile to play a game or watching a YouTube video or going over to the refrigerator to find something delicious to eat. Or it may be internal, just thinking about an interaction with somebody we like, imagining our vacation, etc. All this is wasteful thinking. These are the distractions that help you escape that boredom.

The solution lies in connecting the task to your emotions, and making it seem personally important as well as interesting.

2. Lack of Planning

More often than not, we know which task is most important on our list of tasks, but we keep allowing other less important tasks that *seem* urgent to use up our time. Why does this happen? This is because of poor planning of your time and work, or no planning at all. As Benjamin Franklin once said, *'If you fail to plan, you are planning to fail.'* It is important to understand the difference between important and urgent. We keep on delaying important tasks as they do not seem urgent that very moment. And we attend to tasks that seem urgent, no matter how unimportant they may be. Sumit, in the example mentioned at the beginning of this chapter, did not prioritize the task of writing the proposal and kept taking on other urgent tasks that distracted him from what truly needed to be done then.

So, if we don't categorize our work based on priority, the urgent tasks become a source of distraction from the really important ones we are supposed to be paying attention to. And this finally proves to be counterproductive for us.

3. Negative Bias

Studies show that we tend to focus more on the one negative thought among all the positive ones, which is why we are often not able to concentrate on the right thoughts that help us to complete tasks efficiently.[1]

Rohit was about to leave office when his boss called him to his cabin for some urgent work, which only Rohit could do efficiently. Rohit wanted to refuse but his inability to say 'no' compelled him to do the work. Although he did not have

---

[1]   R. F. Baumeister, E. Bratslavsky, C. Finkenauer and K.D. Vohs, 'Bad Is Stronger Than Good', *Review of General Psychology*, December 2001.

any personal commitments in the evening, he was not happy doing the task. He kept thinking:

> Why am I the only one who is given more responsibilities?
> Why can't I say 'no' to all this extra work?
> Why do people take me for granted?

Such thoughts clouded Rohit's mind. He could have focused on the fact that the boss believed in his efficiency, trusted him, considered him better than others, and Rohit could actually use this time to gain more experience. But the negative thought, 'Why only me?' did not let him concentrate on his work. This affected not only his mental state and his inner peace, but also resulted in his turning in low-quality work.

Researchers believe we tend to have an easier time recalling bad memories than good ones.

Recalling negative events or experiences of the past, and thinking negatively about earlier memories, connects us emotionally to those past events, and as a result, distracts us from our present work. We start visualizing and reliving our past, losing the precious moment of the present.[2]

Have you ever experienced moments when you kept thinking over and over again, of something you did, or what someone did to you? And you felt you were unable to stop thinking about it? The solution is to again find the positive among all the negatives. This is not an easy task, and needs practice and strong determination. It is only possible when

---

[2]   Baumeister, et al, 'Bad Is Stronger Than Good';
      Matthew Killingsworth, and Daniel Gilbert, 'A Wandering Mind is an Unhappy Mind', *Science* 330, no. 932 (2010).

we give ourselves, and pay attention to, the right inputs, i.e., the things we surround ourselves with, what we see, read and listen to should be positive.

4. Discomfort (Physical and Mental)

If you are hungry, uncomfortable, experiencing pain in any part of your body, or feeling cold or very hot, chances are that you won't be able to concentrate on your work. Physical discomfort will continuously distract you from your work. Instead of ignoring these factors, the solution is to remove them and try to be as comfortable as possible when you're working.

On the other hand, mental discomfort can be felt for various reasons, like when you find a task very difficult, or when you doubt your capability to do the task and experience low self-esteem, or when you are not satisfied with the task given to you and so on. Then, it will be difficult for you to concentrate on the work.

Having a comfortable body and a calm state of mind is the only way to do any task in the best possible manner.

Distraction is just another way our brain attempts to deal with mental or physical discomfort of any kind. If we accept this fact, it makes sense that the only way to handle distraction is by learning to handle discomfort.

When I [Aditi] was writing my first book, *How to Become a Human Calculator*, I was struggling to find the right words to put my thoughts on paper. So, every now and then, thoughts of working in the kitchen, or cooking something special for the kids, or making myself a cup of tea, kept distracting me, and I could not sit for a long time to focus on my manuscript. The result was that, for days, I could not complete a single chapter. This made me lose interest in writing, and I developed the belief that the task in itself was very difficult. But then I realized this was a wrong belief and I was somewhere not mentally comfortable with the task of writing, and this was what was not letting me concentrate on the work. I started tackling my wrong belief first. I told myself that I can do this. I encouraged myself by showing myself the bigger purpose and connecting myself emotionally with the task—of helping millions of students through the book. I reinforced the belief that God has chosen me for this task and is empowering me with His powers. I worked on developing my strengths and polishing the skills needed for this task. As my faith in my capabilities grew, so did my interest in writing. Our book *How to Become a Human Calculator* became a bestseller and far exceeded our expectations.

Distractions may not necessarily be your fault,
but managing them is your responsibility.

10

Declutter Your Mind

One day, a bus driver was driving along his usual route. A lot of college students used to board the bus along the route to reach the university. At one of the stops, a tall guy boarded the bus. He had the body of a wrestler and looked strong and intimidating. He was accompanied by a group of boys as strong as him. When the bus conductor asked them to buy tickets, the boy stared at him and rudely said, 'Arjun and his friends don't need to pay.' Having said that, they all took seats at the back of the bus. The short and lightweight conductor looked at the driver for help. The driver didn't argue with Arjun but wasn't happy about it. The next day, the same thing happened—Arjun got on again with his gang, refused to pay and sat down. This went for a few days.

This annoyed the bus driver and the conductor, who started losing sleep over the way Arjun was taking advantage of them. Finally, the bus driver and conductor could not stand it any longer. They started working on their fitness, improved their diet and took help of a bodybuilder to build muscles and learn a few self-defence techniques. After two months, they had become quite strong and felt more confident talking to Arjun.

So, the next time Arjun got on to the bus with his gang and said, 'Arjun and his friends don't need to pay', the conductor stood up, stared back at him, and loudly said, 'And why not?' With a startled look on his face, Arjun replied, 'We have a bus pass.'

Quite often in life we over-evaluate the problems in our mind, thereby making a mountain out of a molehill. Even a tiny problem seems humongous. A simple comment from someone is at times blown out of proportion in our minds, thus taking away our confidence and filling our heart with self-doubt and negativity for the other person. A big part of our life is actually like the above story. We keep making up unnecessary stories, thereby cluttering our mind with negative thoughts.

WHY WE NEED TO DECLUTTER

In the world we live in, we experience digital, physical and mental clutter. With all this clutter, we cannot live the life we want to live. It continuously fogs our thinking and affects our concentration and efficiency. In any situation, if we cannot decide what to do, it means that there is some kind of clutter we are dealing with. Clutter can be equated to **not having clarity**.

Let's say you are having an important discussion on the phone with somebody. All of a sudden, someone starts shouting in the adjoining room, and somebody else switches on the television on full volume. Would you be able to focus on your conversation? No, all this noise will create disturbance and distract you.

In the same way, when too many thoughts are rushing through your mind, thereby generating a lot of unnecessary signals in your brain, they rob you of your ability to think clearly. Your ability to make decisions drops drastically. A calm mind is the wellspring of concentration, and anything that disturbs the stillness of the mind reduces your ability to focus. It can be a single event that you recall from the past, an event that you are afraid of facing in the future or even something totally unrelated.

TECHNIQUES TO DECLUTTER YOUR MIND

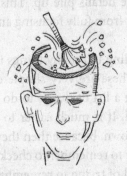

We often download a lot of things online to watch later but rarely get the time to go back to them again. When downloads become excessive, they take up all the storage space on our device. We start facing various issues with our device, like slow functioning, etc. How do we fix this? We start deleting files that now seem unnecessary, to ensure our device runs smoothly. Unfortunately, the challenge lies in applying the same technique to our minds, to ensure our brains also run smoothly.

We all know exactly what we need to download on or delete from our smartphones. It is time we learn to do the same for our mind. Here are a few simple techniques to declutter your mind.

1. Pen and Paper Kit

Most people try using their memory to keep track of all the things they need to do and places they need to be. But the fact is that you simply cannot rely on your memory alone to keep track of all these details without it getting overloaded, as our working memory is very limited. Keeping track of too many things in the mind leads to anxiety—you begin to feel overwhelmed as the details pile up. This causes distraction, which prevents you from fully focusing and concentrating on your work.

Instead of juggling too many things in your mind, use a *paper* and a *pen*. These are very simple devices to declutter your brain. Making a list of things to do will reduce a lot of your cognitive load. It is much easier to plan and prioritize by writing things down, because then they can be compared. Now, you only have to remember to check your list and check things off it, instead of trying to remember all the things that need to be done and getting confused in the details.

2. Constraints on Choices

This is the bane of our modern society—in every single area, you have a bunch of choices to make. What once might have been a ten-minute trip to grab necessities now requires at least that much time to agonize over the best brand of detergent or the right shampoo to suit the texture of your hair. Even if you want to buy a pair of jeans, you will be faced with an endless array of decisions. You have to choose among straight fit, skinny fit, flared, boot cut and so on and so forth. And the colour choices are even more. So many choices clutter your mind, and trying to make a decision can become too exhausting. This is what leads to what psychologists call *continuous partial satisfaction*. Even after making a decision, you are never fully happy. You always feel maybe you should have explored one more shop.

Psychologist Barry Schwartz coined the phrase '**paradox of choice**', which sums up his findings that increased choice leads to greater anxiety, indecision, paralysis and dissatisfaction.[1] More choices might afford objectively better results, but they won't make you happy.

He suggests that you should impose constraints when you have to choose something. For example, if you have to buy certain things from the mall, impose some kind of constraints. These constraints can be, 'I will not consider anything that costs more than three thousand rupees' or 'I will not spend more than half an hour searching for this particular item'. Constraints of these sorts help us to reduce the number of choices, which in turn helps us to reduce the clutter.

Steve Jobs, Mark Zuckerberg and even Barack Obama made the decision to limit their clothing options to save

---

[1] B. Schwartz, A. Ward, J. Monterosso, S. Lyubomirsky, K. White, D.R. Lehman, 'Maximizing versus Satisficing: Happiness is a Matter of Choice', *Journal of Personality and Social Psychology* 83, no. 5 (November, 2002):1178-97.

their time and minimize feelings of being overwhelmed from making too many decisions. In an interview, Obama said, 'You'll see I wear only gray or blue suits. I am trying to pare down decisions about what I'm eating or wearing, because I have too many other decisions to make.'

> *The key is deciding what you want, what is important to you, and then sticking to it.*

3. Change Your Perception, Change Your Life

To understand what perception is, and how it affects your life, let's look at this picture.

Carefully describe what you see.

Do you see a ship? What else you can see on it? What other symbols or things can you see around it? You probably would describe clouds in the sky, water under the ship, a person sitting on the left end of the ship playing an instrument, the rising sun.

But what if we were to tell you that this illustration is of a face of a person with his eyes open, wearing a hat, with a pipe in his mouth, a cup of hot beverage, and the digits 1, 2, 3, 4, 5 and 6 written roughly at the bottom? Doesn't seem like it, does it?

Now look at the picture again.

It is the same picture turned upside down.

So, what changed, if not the picture?

What you see (*your perception*) is your reality, and that is governed by how you look at things (*your perspective*). The *way* you look at things determines the nature of your experiences.

Things are going to remain as they are. They will not change. Your son will not change; your mother-in-law will not change; your daughter-in-law will not change; nor will your difficult boss or the job that requires you to work too much. They will be who they are and things will remain the way they are. If you have to reduce the clutter the situations and people in your life are causing, you will have to change *your perspective*.

Once, a salesman from a renowned shoe company went to a remote country to determine the market potential of their products. After his survey, he reported to his senior that 'No one here wears any shoes! There is no market for us here!' As he was about to leave for his country, he saw an old man limping on hot sand. His feet were cracked, and he was in great pain. He thought how great it would be if he could help the old man by giving him a pair of shoes. This gave him an idea. He sent a new message to his senior, 'No one here wears any shoes! There is a huge market for us!' The moment he changed his perspective, he could see new opportunities in the same scenario.

If I can change the way I look at things,
I can change the things I look at.

4. Edit Your Own Narrative

We all are experts at creating stories in our minds. When the actual situation could be summarized in maybe just two lines, we often end up making a two-page narrative out of it. And most of the script would consist of what we feel others are thinking about us.

Rajiv is a sincere and dedicated employee who loves his job. But his new boss has been a reason for his uneasiness and discomfort in office for the last few months. Rajiv has noticed his boss double-checking the reports that he submits before forwarding them to the main office. This has really stressed him out, and he is not able to enjoy his work the way he used to. He feels that his boss doesn't trust him and doubts his capabilities. He thinks his boss is always finding faults with his work. This has taken a toll on his confidence.

What is the objective reality in the above situation? It is just that his boss always double-checks his work. The rest of it is a narrative Rajiv has built up in his head.

In most cases of mental cluttering, the cluttering does not happen due to the actual situation. It always happens because of such narratives you are telling yourself about the actual situation. It is your opinion about others, your own insecurities, and creating your own alternate reality about what actually happened that mostly creates unnecessary clutter and thereby stress. Stress in your life is a result of mental clutter. Now, as an observer, see your own story. Just delete all the imaginary script from your story. It will come down to only one or two lines. Only if you take charge of the clutter will you be able to delete it.

You might have created many long narratives about past events in your life and kept them stored in your memory. It is your responsibility to edit and remove the clutter from them so they become as close as possible to reality.

5. Be Non-Judgemental

Listening is a quality that is very rare. We assume things without even giving other people a chance to speak. In a conversation, we build up on cues and form images in our head, and assume things that might not be true. We reach a conclusion even before the other person has finished their part of the conversation. Our judgements can be a big barrier to listening.

Our bad past experiences and future worries leave a deep impression on our minds and make us assume things that might not be true. A call from a friend who had borrowed money from you many times in the past makes you think that he has called for the same purpose, even though he may be calling to invite you for dinner.

When we see our child coming to us, we assume that he is going to make a demand, as this has been a pattern in the past. All he does is comes and gives us a hug. The real reason might be a problem bothering him.

It is important that you must first listen with an open mind, analyse, and only then come to a conclusion. Don't assume things and create unnecessary clutter, as reality may be completely different. Detach your mind from bad past experiences and from the fear of things happening the same way in the future. Live in the present and judge things accordingly.

We hope the techniques discussed in this chapter will empower you to declutter your mind and thus bring peace and contentment to your life.

If we cannot organize our mind,
we cannot organize our life.

11

Asking the Right Questions

A teacher conducting a lesson on the digestive system with his Class 5 students asked one of them:

'How long is the oesophagus?'
'I have no idea,' he responded.
The teacher hadn't told them this fact yet.
'You have *no* idea?' the teacher questioned again.
'None,' the student replied.
'Well then, could it be a kilometre long?' the teacher asked.
'Of course not,' the student responded.
'How about an inch long?'
'No way.'
'So you *do* have some idea about how long an oesophagus is,' the teacher reminded him.
She went on to ask, 'So, can you then tell me *where* the oesophagus is?'
'It runs from our throat to our stomach,' the student quickly answered.

'How long is that?'

'About a foot and a half!'

Asking the right question resulted in the correct answer.

The key to powerful thinking is powerful questioning. When we ask the right questions, we succeed as a thinker, for questions act as the force that give direction to our thinking. Wherever your question leads, your attention follows. Wherever your attention goes, your thoughts flow. That's the reason it's important to explore the power of questions.

Questions help to

- give a direction to the thought process.
- shut off all unnecessary thoughts, at least temporarily, as you are focused on answering the question.
- increase the observation power.
- improve our attention and concentration.

ROLE OF 'QUESTIONS' IN INNOVATION

Questions spark curiosity in your mind. Curiosity leads to new ideas, and new ideas lead to *innovation*. It was Aryabhatta's question 'What is the shape of earth?' that led to the discovery that the earth is round and not flat.

When we looked closer at some innovations, we were surprised to see how many began with asking the right questions.

- *Why does an apple fall to the earth and not rise towards the sky?*

  Apples had been falling from trees and on many people since time immemorial, but when Newton stopped to pay attention to the phenomenon and asked himself this question, it led to the theory of gravitation.

- *How do birds fly in the sky and not us? How can I fly?*
  This led to the invention of aircraft and rockets, and enabled us to conquer the sky and reach the moon.

- *Who am I? Is there a God? What is the purpose of life?*
  The quest to answer these important questions led to all the world's greatest philosophies and religions.

- *What would DNA look like in 3D form?*
  When Watson and Crick asked this question, they were able to discover the double-helix structure of the DNA.

- *How can I get a good burger on the road?*
  The search led Ray Kroc to establish McDonald's.

- *What can be done about the mounting number of landfills? Can they be used to benefit society at large?*
  In 2008, twelve-year-old Max Wallack of Massachusetts created a 'Home-Dome', a Mongolian yurt-shaped structure made of waste plastic filled with styrofoam packing peanuts. This was designed to serve as a temporary shelter for homeless people and disaster victims. What it also aimed to do was to stem the growth of landfills.

Every innovation or invention is an answer. Everything you do and everything you're surrounded by every day is actually an answer to a specific question. It's either a why, what, how, who or where.

The answers to each of the questions mentioned above may have taken a lot of time, but the foundation for each beautiful creation started with a question. So, the next time any social or global problem catches your attention, such as water scarcity, increasing pollution and global warming, don't just pass judgement or comments. Instead, ask yourself some pertinent questions, which may lead you to some innovative solutions.

You might argue that you do not have the technical or scientific expertise to tackle that problem. You will be surprised to know that the same Max Wallack who created 'Home Dome', designed wooden steps with a handle to help his great grandmother get into automobiles, when he was only in Class 2. What expertise do you think he had at that age? What actually led to the invention was his mindset of 'How can I help?'

Always ask yourself 'What can *I* do to solve this issue?' Your effort, no matter how small, can lead to something big, inspiring many others to do their bit.

THE RIGHT QUESTIONS LEAD TO THE RIGHT SOLUTIONS

'If I had an hour to solve a problem and my life depended on the solution, I would spend the first 55 minutes determining the proper question to ask, for once I know the proper question, I could solve the problem in less than five minutes.'

Albert Einstein

The kind of answers we are going to get depend a lot on the kind of questions we ask. A question, if asked in the correct way, can direct our attention straight to the solutions, whereas the same question asked in a different way can be disempowering, forcing us to look at more problems instead. Let's understand this with an example. Suppose you always wake up late and are not able to get things done on time. You probably ask yourself: *Why do I always oversleep?*

Such questions are problem-centric and energy-sapping because there can be many reasons why you oversleep. Your question is directing you to focus on the problem and not the solution. Such questions are disempowering and make you believe that you are the problem.

Instead, you can rephrase the question as '*How can I get up early?*'

Notice the difference. The answer you are looking for is in asking how to wake up early. The first question is giving you reasons you were oversleeping. The moment you flip the question and ask yourself 'How can I get up early?' you start exploring ways to solve your problem. Such questions are empowering and lead you to the solutions. They direct your thoughts towards positive outcomes.

> *Empowering questions are the ones that are solution-centric and energize you.*

Similarly, instead of asking an employee '*Why are you always late?*', it would be more productive to ask '*How can I help you make sure you come on time from tomorrow?*'

Where a good question has the power to give direction to one's thinking, a poor question can sometimes hamper the thought process. When a teacher asks a student 'What is 6×6?' and the student answers '34', the teacher can snap at the student, make them feel small and say, 'How can you give such a silly answer; 6×6 is 36. You don't know even this much!'

By doing this, the teacher has discouraged the student from volunteering to answer in the future. The same situation can be handled in a very simple way by the teacher, where they can ask, *'Can you please explain how?'*

The student will most likely realize the mistake and reach the correct answer. Most importantly, we will get to know how the child arrived at an incorrect answer, at which step they were making an error, and then accordingly guide them to the right solution.

Also note that when the teacher shows curiosity, the **question becomes a beautiful tool of empowerment and learning for the student**. The next time, the student will happily raise their hand to give an answer because they know that even if they are wrong, the teacher is not going to snap. We need to remodel the way we teach and the way we ask students, or anyone for that matter, questions. They need to be in the form of these open-ended questions that help to encourage better learning and creativity.

But one important thing should be kept in mind. When you ask a question, you should give some time to the other person to think about their answer. Generally, it is a second or two. But allowing the person a minimum of 5 seconds can actually increase the probability of them answering correctly.

Several studies from the 1970s have looked into the effect that the amount of time teachers pause after asking a question has on learners. With few exceptions, these studies are still accurate. For example, according to work done by Mary Budd Rowe in 1972 and Robert J. Stahl in 1994, pausing for three or more seconds showed a noticeably positive impact on learning. Yet the average length that teachers pause after asking a question was found to be 0.9 seconds.[1]

QUESTIONS LEADERS SHOULD ASK

You can tell whether a man is clever by his answers.
You can tell whether a man is wise by his questions.

In the current world where we strive for equality and parity, leaders don't communicate in monologues, they encourage conversations. They don't treat their team meetings as a war that they want to win; rather, they take them as opportunities to teach and learn at the same time.

What is the best tool to achieve this? Questions.

A capable leader is a person who asks the right questions to the right person at the right time.

*How can I get the **most** out of my team?*

That's a typical thought in a manager's mind. But a manager who is a good leader thinks:

*How can I get the **best** out of my team?*

Notice the difference. Sincere asking demonstrates a willingness to guide, a desire to serve, and a humility that can

---

[1] John McCarthy, 'Extending the Silence', Edutopia.com, 10 January 2018, https://www.edutopia.org/article/extending-silence;

J. Robert Stahl, 'Using "Think-Time" and "Wait-Time" Skillfully in the Classroom. ERIC Digest', Eric.ed.gov.com, May 1994, , https://files.eric.ed.gov/fulltext/ED370885.pdf

be an inspiration for the entire organization. Just changing one word in the question reorients the attention. Suddenly, the manager starts noticing and respecting the team's capabilities. The most beautiful thing in leaders and managers is *sincere asking*.

One of our friends, who is a teacher in a school, shared an experience that exemplifies the role of a good leader. The principal of the school asked some of the teachers to prepare some activities for students, such as contests, quizzes and skits, on the topic 'Changing values of our society'. The principal herself decided to lead the team of ten teachers. The teachers were not too happy about the extra work as they already had their hands full. Unwillingly, they went to the principal's chamber and braced themselves for a list of imposed responsibilities. But to their astonishment, instead of the principal delegating work to them, she asked them, 'What contribution would you like to make in your individual capacity?' As a result, the teachers felt motivated to choose their duties. Immediately, they started introspecting on their strengths. With a happy heart, they decided on a range of exciting activities. As they were playing to their strengths, it did not seem like a burden to them, and they planned the week with great energy and excitement.

The teachers were surprised to see how students participated in all the activities with enthusiasm. Everything went off smoothly without any stress. The events were well appreciated by the parents, who felt the topic around which the programmes were conducted was highly relevant. It was possible for all this to be set in motion by one carefully framed question by the principal, which gave the right direction to the whole task. The question turned out to be one of the main reasons for the success.

This art of sincere asking made the team members engage as one and helped the principal become the best leader that she could. That's why today's leaders know how to unlock the hidden qualities and bring out the best in others through well-timed, well-framed, empathetic questions.

An organization wanted to be the best in the world in its field. It started a huge campaign all over the globe and encouraged their employees to send in their ideas on how they could make the organization the best in the world. One day, one of the engineers approached the marketing head and said that the campaign didn't inspire him. He said:

We are thinking about:

'How can we make our organization the best *in* the world?'

We should think:

'How can we make our organization the best *for* the world?'

It was an eye-opener for the manager, and he started approaching things differently. The employees started approaching local communities and started asking questions on how their company could help them. They wanted to know how the people around them could harness the company's knowledge and power. By helping locals solve their problems, they created a billion-dollar business! Today, the company is known as Hewlett Packard (HP).

In our competitive world, the thoughts that rule our mind are how to be the best in the team, the best in the class or the best in the country. Just for one month, try to be the best *for* the team. See the joy and success you get from it.

QUESTIONS TO ASK YOURSELF

What type of conversations do you have with yourself? Do you berate yourself and act as your own worst critic? Do you spend any time on what you have done or achieved and what you are capable of doing? How about you take some time out for self-appreciation and ask yourself what you are good at?

You are not a bundle of weaknesses but of strengths! You don't have to overcome each weakness. Rather, you can start exploring the beauty inside you, your virtues and the goodness of your heart.

The Queue of Wrong Whys:

Why does this always happen with me? What will others think of me? Why did I do this? If we dwell on such questions, one 'why' will lead to another.

Jealousy, anger and depression all start with the wrong question: What does she think of herself? Why is he not working the way I want? Why don't I have what he has? This leads to a downward spiral.

Curiosity, however, leads to an upward spiral: How does the system work? What are the areas in which I need to improve? What are my good qualities? What has he done to achieve all that he has today? Confidence, harmony and empathy start with asking the right question.

Every negative thing you experience starts with the wrong question. Every positive thing you experience starts with the right question.

Questions draw attention and wherever attention goes, energy flows and it encourages growth. Your attention may be on the wrong things, as your questions may not be correctly framed.

Asking questions means there is a desire to understand things further. Thinking is not driven by answers. It is driven by questions. The minute you get an answer, you stop thinking. It's a question that always stimulates thinking, not the answer.

Imagine you planned to spend an hour on the phone and then start preparing for an upcoming exam, but you ended up spending two hours instead. Now you are regretting the loss of self-control.

Instead of asking yourself, 'Why did I waste my time?' ask, 'How can I utilize the remaining time in the best possible manner?' But it does not end there. You also need to pay attention to your self-control at the same time, so you don't waste time again.

Introspect, 'In what ways can I overcome this addiction to my phone?'

Just concentrating on our weaknesses takes away our confidence. We need to concentrate on our strengths and look for ways to use those strengths to work on our weaknesses.

HOW MEDITATION HELPS IN QUESTIONING

Your quality of life depends on the quality of decisions you make and the quality of decisions depends on the quality of questions you ask. The quality of questions in turn depends on the quality of your thinking. Meditation helps improve the quality of your thinking. Meditation requires you to sit back and remind yourself of your inner beauty, your inner treasure.

The Relationship between Meditation and Questions

Deep and significant learning happens only as a result of reflection. Reflection is not possible without asking questions. Great sages, scientists and leaders always spent time reflecting on themselves, reflecting on situations, reflecting on questions. Whether the question is from an external or internal source, deep reflection and introspection causes significant learning. It helps create the space to evaluate various alternatives dispassionately. It improves your ability to appreciate and accept.

During my student life, when I [Aditi] used to see others speaking on stage, I used to ask myself, 'How can I be as good as them?' That made me believe that I was not as talented, and I used to feel inferior to them. Years later, when I started practising Raja Yoga meditation, I realized that I always kept asking myself the wrong questions, which led me to comparing myself with others. Then, I redirected my attention by asking myself 'What am I good at? What are my strengths?' and then I started finding a treasure of potential inside me that had been hidden for so many years.

Meditation helps develop non-judgemental awareness and improves your decision-making. Work towards becoming non-judgemental; don't get carried away by your emotions; and learn to detach yourself from the situation and have an objective view. Focus on the facts of the situation and not on the narrative you are telling yourself about the fact. When the focus is on your own narrative, you get upset. When the focus is on facts, you think about better solutions. This non-judgemental awareness helps you to shift your focus from the story you are telling yourself to the objective facts in the situation.

Meditation helps you to let go. When you fail, it helps you accept that you failed and also helps you understand that *you* are not a failure. You can always learn and improve. Meditation helps you take control of yourself. Take charge of your inner self before taking charge of things outside you.

In your habit of asking wrong questions—like 'What more do I need?'—you forget what you already have. Take some time to ask yourself, 'What are the ten things that I feel grateful for in my life right now?'

Now ask yourself, 'What would I do differently at the workplace or home if I knew I couldn't fail or be criticized?'

Whether you are aware or not, you are constantly failing at asking yourself the right questions. So, if you want to change your life, change your questions. That is where it all begins.

EXERCISE

Now that you know the importance of asking the right questions, it's time to get out of the habit of wrong questioning. Like any other skill, this requires practice. Here are some wrong questions that we often ask. We have converted a few of them to the right ones. Try to reframe the rest.

Wrong Question	Right Question
Why do I spend too much time on phone playing games?	How can I utilize my time better?
Why do I get distracted so easily?	What should I do to improve my concentration?
Why don't people listen to me?	
Why don't my children respect me?	
Why don't my employees work with dedication?	
Why am I not achieving my targets?	
How do people cheat me so easily?	
Why am I so short-tempered?	
Will I always have a mediocre life?	
When will the environment get better?	

SUGGESTED RIGHT QUESTIONS

Wrong Question	Right Question
Why do I spend too much time on phone, playing games?	How can I utilize my time better?
Why do I get distracted so easily?	What should I do to improve my concentration?
Why don't people listen to me?	How can I improve my communication skills?
Why don't my children respect me?	How can I set a good example for my children so that they respect me?
Why don't my employees work with dedication?	What should I do to motivate my employees?
Why am I not reaching my targets?	How should I plan to attain my targets?
How can people cheat me so easily?	How can I be more vigilant?
Why am I so short-tempered?	What should I do to control my temper?
Will I always have a mediocre life?	How can I improve the quality of my life?
When will the environment get better?	What can I do to make the environment better?

12

High-Calorie Digital Consumption

Digital technology has been a force for the good in both our personal and professional lives. But as you know, too much of anything is bad. You may like sugar a lot but you cannot keep having it as much as you want. And what will happen if you do? Consumption of more calories than you burn will make you overweight and adversely affect your body. Similarly, over-consumption of a '**high-calorie' digital diet** from the Internet can affect your brain and thought process as well as your emotional and physical well-being. It is a major source of distraction in your day-to-day life and has made concentrating on something a rare skill.

> *By paying attention to your distractions,*
> *you are distracting your attention.*
> *Learn to ignore your distraction,*
> *if you want to pay attention.*

DIGITAL ACCESS AND AFFORDABILITY

Just a decade ago, when mobile phones became prevalent, you would switch on the mobile data to log on to the Internet and then switch it off. Or you would wait for a Wi-Fi hotspot. Now those days are gone, and you can create your own hotspots! The ease of accessibility that this has provided has at the same time multiplied your distractions.

Research on Internet usage by the investment firm Omidyar Network suggests that on an average, a user in India spends 200 minutes a day on mobile apps, which is lower than the US average of 300 minutes a day. But Indians spend almost 70 per cent of this time on social media apps, such as Facebook, WhatsApp and Instagram, and other music and entertainment apps, whereas people in the US spend only 50 per cent of their time on such apps.[1] Now this is where you are spending a major part of your life. Think back to how much time you used to spend on your phone just three or four years ago. Isn't there a marked increase in how much time you spend on the Internet today?

Service providers give free access to millions of songs, more than 1,00,000 hours of movies (if you watch these for 10 hours a day, you'll finish in about thirty years), more than 400 TV channels, and hundreds of digital magazines and newspapers. Every week, so many more movies, tele-series

---

[1]   Shalina Pillai, 'Indians Spend 70% of Mobile Internet Time on Social Media, Entertainment', TimesofIndia.indiatimes.com, 19 December 2017, https://timesofindia.indiatimes.com/business/india-business/indians-spend-70-of-mobile-internet-time-on-social-entertainment/articleshow/62125840.cms

and reality shows are added, all for free. And we proudly celebrate that India has been in the lead in mobile usage.

Accessible Data + Affordable Data = Loads of Digital Calories

Distraction has become a lot more affordable. So, there are a few simple questions that you need to reflect on. How much time are you spending on your devices? Is it productive? Is it necessary or even useful?

High-calorie digital consumption and information absorption is impacting our brain, productivity and relationships.

IMPACT ON OUR BRAIN

A researcher called Gary Small scanned the brains of a bunch of people while they were browsing content on the Internet and then again as they were reading the same content in a book.[2]

The scanned brain images showed that when you are reading a book, only some parts of the brain are activated, whereas when you are surfing the Internet, more parts of the brain are activated.[3] The prefrontal cortex, where we make decisions and analyse things, was prominently lit up. When

---

[2] Gary Small and Gigi Vorgan, *iBrain: Surviving the Technological Alteration of the Modern Mind* (New York: Collins, 2008), pp. 14–17.

[3] G. W. Small, T. D. Moody, P. Siddarth, and S. Y. Bookheimer, 'Your Brain on Google: Patterns of Cerebral Activation during Internet Searching,' *American Journal of Geriatric Psychiatry* 17, no. 2 (February 2009): 116–26.

you read content online, you have to make decisions every few seconds—should I click this link or should I skip it?—because you are invariably browsing through pages that have hyperlinks. Studies show that this mode of reading does not give you enough opportunity to absorb the big picture and integrate what you are reading with existing concepts in your memory.[4] This continuous decision-making consumes a significant amount of your mental energy.

When you are reading a book, you only have to decide between two options, to continue reading or to stop. There is nothing else to decide. This gives you more brain space and therefore a better chance to absorb the information.

IMPACT ON OUR PRODUCTIVITY AND GROWTH

We often do multiple things at the same time in life, but more so while using our smartphones. We check our WhatsApp messages, go to YouTube links, answer emails, browse Instagram, check notifications and so on and so forth. Not just that, we take pride in admitting that we can operate multiple apps and communicate with various people at one time. But researchers have found that if you continue to use your mobile phone like this, it will not be of much good and will hugely impact your productivity.[5] That's why more often than not, you forget to attach files while sending emails, click

---

[4]   Erping Zhu, 'Hypermedia Interface Design: The Effects of Number of Links and Granularity of Nodes,' *Journal of Educational Multimedia and Hypermedia*, 8, no. 3 (1999): 331–58.

[5]   Melina R. Uncapher, Anthony D. Wagner, 'Media Multitasking, Mind, and Brain', *Proceedings of the National Academy of Sciences* 115, no.40 (Oct 2018), 9889–9896.

on 'Like' buttons without intending to, click on useless links, add a wrong amount to your e-wallet and send the wrong emoticons.

When you open too many apps on your mobile, it slows down its performance. This is because your mobile uses a portion of its processing power to switch between the apps. When this switching increases, the amount of processing power available for running the apps reduces. The brain functions in the same way. When you are engaged in one activity and you want to switch to another activity, you have to pay a **switching penalty.** And if you don't give enough time for this switching, your mental processes, like a computer, can crash. If you keep switching among tasks without giving your brain enough time to focus on one particular activity, to start enjoying and experiencing it, your ability to experience the world drastically falls. You experience **continuous partial attention**; that is, being in a distracted state at all times. It is extremely harmful for your mental health.

A distracted and constantly stimulated brain is a weak and stressed brain.

Check with yourself: When was the last time you took 15 minutes of your time just for yourself, to speak to yourself? We don't seem to have that kind of time at all. It is not just grown-ups who suffer from the disorder of continuous partial attention. Kids face this at a much younger age. Their decreasing attention spans are leading to poor school performance, anxiety and depression. Obesity and sleep disorders have also seen a rise because of the increasing amount of time spent online, which not only leads to a sedentary lifestyle but also upsets sleep schedules. There are teenagers in South Korea who wear adult diapers while playing online games so that they don't have to get up for nature's call! Such is the level of their addiction.

> *When you keep chopping your attention, you are not able to focus. It increases your anxiety, your discontentment, and subsequently, reduces your productivity.*

IMPACT ON OUR RELATIONSHIPS AND FAMILY

As the use of digital technology has increased, so have the levels of impatience in the present generation. It is because they have become used to the *instant* gratification that the digital world offers. There was a time when we would order something and patiently wait for its arrival. Now, when we order something, we impatiently wait for it to arrive at the earliest. **Patience** has been replaced with **Impatience**. Technology has made us used to instant gratification, and this is one of the key reasons for many mental health issues. We don't give ourselves time. We are no longer patient. We want it *now*; we cannot wait. This is reflecting even in our relationships. First, we don't give attention to our children when they need us, as we are busy replying to a text or returning a call or writing an email. When we see our children doing the same to us, we feel annoyed and reprimand them. This can distance us from our kids, and it often gets blamed on generation gap. But the truth is that we no longer give our relationships time to mature because impatience is seeping into every single aspect of our lives. These are all complex problems and need distinctive and creative solutions. However, such creative solutions are not possible without deep, reflective and introspective thinking and the willingness to change.

So here are a few things to ponder over:

What are you doing at any given time? Where and how are you spending most of your time? Are you spending time on things that *seem* essential but may not actually be healthy for your mind? Are these things really that essential? What kind of example are you setting for your kids? Do you greet your loved ones with your loving and attentive face or has it been replaced by the top of our heads as you constantly stare into your mobile screen?

13

Life on Social Media

It felt like a knife had pierced through Pranay's heart when he saw pictures of his friend on an online platform. His newly married friend, Arnav, was holidaying at an exotic location with his gorgeous wife, Ritu. Pranay's search for a partner had taken longer than anticipated, and pictures like these made him feel lonelier and more frustrated.

Next month, this newly married couple saw a picture of Pranay on his social media account where he was standing next to the latest model of an SUV, beaming with pride. They burned with jealously as they were facing a financial crunch after having spent a bomb on their honeymoon and could not afford a car right now.

After a week, their common friends (Sandeep and Riya) posted lovely pictures of their new apartment with hashtags like #madly in love and #heaven on earth. In reality, the couple was going through a rough patch in their marriage. They were fighting a lot and on the verge of separation. But when they moved into their new apartment, they posted a picture to find some gratification and solace in showing it off to others.

But their display of 'affection' took away all the love and excitement from the life of the newly wedded Arnav and Ritu, who now felt their own apartment was not good enough, and started fighting over other petty issues.

Pranay, who had purchased a car only to overcompensate for his insecurities of not being able to buy a house or find a partner, broke down when he saw his friends' pictures.

Doesn't this happen with all of us at one point or another? Isn't this the way we all feel? We judge people by their amazing pictures on social media, where they showcase their travel plans, new house, car, phone or even their new pair of shoes. Every other day, you will find pictures of people partying at the most 'happening' places. But does anyone put up a picture of their hangover the next day? Do they ever post about the EMIs they are paying for that car or house or even vacations?

These updates of other people's lives take away your own concentration on your life, your goals, your relationships and things that hold importance in your life. Instead, you start paying more attention to others' lives and their goals and activities. This constant comparison fills you with negativity, insecurity and jealousy. Deep in your heart you know that it's not real, but as soon as you see a new post, you go green with envy. Social media is like a deep ocean where you only see the surface. You cannot see what lies below the surface of people's lives. The adverse effects of this social-media obsession can lead to a lot of issues, like isolation, loneliness, broken relationships and torn families. As we mentioned in earlier chapters, what you pay attention to determines the quality of your life. If you develop such strong negative feelings while browsing social media, you create barriers to your goals as well as to your achievements.

IMPACT OF SOCIAL MEDIA

A newspaper article caught our attention a few months ago. It was about a man who wanted to divorce his wife as she spent sixteen hours a day on Facebook. He complained that she ignored their kids too, because of which he had to send them to a hostel. But even then, she did not change. And that's why he did not want to stay in that marriage anymore.

These networking platforms were designed to reconnect us with long-lost friends and follow up on other relationships, both personal and professional, but they have instead led to discontentment and disconnection. Earlier, when there used to be only one landline phone in the house, our hearts were more connected. Whenever a loved one called, we would all gather around the phone to overhear or join in the conversation. We were more in touch with our loved ones.

But now, with a cell phone in everyone's hand, though we are more socially 'connected' with others, we have become disconnected with the things happening in the lives of our own family members. Even while having dinner, though we sit together, we are not with each other. Our thoughts are in a faraway world full of virtual friends.

We have become hi-tech in our connections with other people but have lost the art of physical meetings full of warmth and attentiveness. Social media has taken students not just away from family but from books as well. They don't realize that the phones they use come with another **SIM**— Stress In Mind!

A report by the Royal Society for Public Health states that social media usage is related to enhanced rates of anxiety, depression, poor sleep quality, body image issues and cyberbullying. In fact, rates of anxiety and depression in young people have increased by 70 per cent in the last twenty-five years. Body image issues are a problem for both genders, but nine in ten teenage girls say that they are unhappy with their body. Seven out of ten teens have experienced cyberbullying, and 37 per cent say they experience it very frequently. The report also says that Facebook, Twitter, Instagram and Snapchat have an overall adverse effect on the well-being of the younger generation.[1]

Of course, totally avoiding social media is not a practical solution today. But we need to do everything we can to not get affected by this illusionary world that people are creating. Don't judge their state of life by what they display on these platforms. Don't borrow their goals from them and lose sight of your own. A trip to the snow-clad mountains in Manali might not give you the same happiness as it gives them. Just because a cousin bought a new car, don't suddenly start looking at your car with disgust and inadequacy. Just feel happy for them and concentrate on the things in your life that are a reason for your happiness.

In case you feel tempted to post something online, pause and reflect. Is this really necessary? Do I really want to share this with the world? Will it bring happiness to even one person's life in this world? The answer to these questions will make you go back on your thought about nine out of ten times.

Don't use online platforms to impress people; use it to impact people.

[1] '#StatusofMind', Royal Society of Public Health, May 2017, https://www.rsph.org.uk/our-work/campaigns/status-of-mind.html

14

E-Diseases and Their Remedies

You must have heard many people telling you about the harmful effects of long and continuous use of mobile phones. Now let's explore the reality behind those claims. **E-diseases** is the term we have given to the diseases that are a result of new technologies. In this chapter, we go into detail of the ways in which we have been impacted by these E-Diseases.

LIST OF E-DISEASES

Disturbed Sleep

- Our devices emit a blue light, which disturbs our sleep cycles by tricking the brain, saying that it is not yet time to go to sleep. This impacts secretion of melatonin, which signals to the brain that night has arrived and we should sleep. The resultant lack of sleep, affects our concentration, makes us prone to mistakes and impairs our memory the next day. By disturbing melatonin secretion and our sleep cycles, the smartphone light can also mess with the hormones that manage our appetite, potentially increasing the risk of either obesity or weight loss.

Remedy

You can install certain applications like Flux and Twilight on your mobile. A lot of phones offer automatic blue light filters as well. These apps turn the screen colours a yellowish red and orange, from blue, thereby reducing the impact on melatonin secretion.

Loss of Vision

Reading text of small size on your smartphone can affect your vision permanently. This happens as your eyes are strained constantly by the blue light emanating from the smartphone. Reading or browsing on your smartphones in absence of external light further complicates the problem.

- How many of you use eye drops for lubricating your eyes when they dry up after prolonged screen time?
- How many of you suffer headaches?

That's because we have forgotten the habit of blinking. The simple act of blinking lubricates the eyes—something we forget to do while staring at our screens. This causes our eyes to itch and burn and leads to dry eyes, and from there, headaches; in worst cases, it may even lead to blurred vision.

Remedy

- You need to follow the 20–20–20 rule to limit the harmful effects on your eyes. Every 20 minutes, for 20 seconds, look at something that is 20 feet away.
- Blink often to lubricate the eyes.

Text Neck

You tend to bend your head forward for long periods of time to look down at your phone. This prolonged bad posture results in rounded shoulders, and upper and lower back pain. This condition is known as 'text neck'. When you are standing or sitting straight, your head puts a load of about 10–12 lb (5.5 kg approx.) on your neck. When texting on a phone, you generally bend the head forward and look down at a 45–60 degree angle, , this increases the weight on your neck five times! It's as if you're putting an additional 27 kg weight on your neck and this is what leads to text neck. This problem is particularly more disturbing because children of the growing age also have easy access to mobiles and tablets, and such postures can lead to lifelong neck issues. It's time we become conscious of how many times and how many minutes a day do you do this? And what is it leading to? The answer to the last question is headaches, neck and shoulder pain, low back problems, difficulty in breathing and pain in the chest.

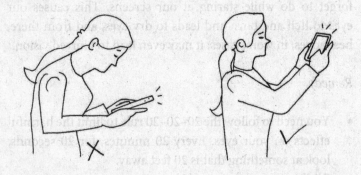

Remedy

- When you're texting, hold the phone at eye level. It may be a bit uncomfortable, but you're saving yourself from a lot of neck and back pain. It may also help limit your usage and encourage you to think about your actions more carefully.
- Do regular neck strengthening exercises.

Cell-Phone Elbow

Like tennis elbow, you can also get cell-phone elbow. When you hold your mobile phone for long periods, the ulnar nerve, which is underneath the elbow and controls your ring and little fingers, gets stretched. As this nerve is stretched, blood supply to it gets restricted and you may experience numbness and tingling. This condition is known as cell-phone elbow (Cubital Tunnel Syndrome). If it gets severe, you may even need surgery.

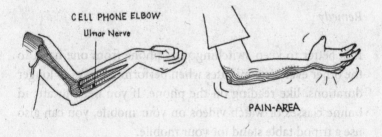

Remedy

Give your phone and elbow some rest. Don't indulge in long chats over your mobile phone. Limit usage and take breaks.

Wrist Issues

- When people hold their phone in their left hand, they usually use the last three fingers and the thumb while using the forefinger of the right hand to tap on the screen. Contorting our fingers and our hand for long durations every day, in such a manner, tends to cause pain in the wrist.

Remedy

It is better to keep switching your phone from one hand to the other every few minutes when performing tasks of longer durations, like reading on the phone. If you need to attend online classes or watch videos on your mobile, you can also use a tripod table stand for your mobile.

Text Claw

Not only texting, but too much browsing can also give you a text claw. It can create soreness and cramping in your fingers, wrist and forearm. If you have thumb pain and have to take breaks to rest your thumbs while using your smartphone, you might already be suffering from text claw. Other symptoms are pain in the hand or wrist when bending or straightening the thumb.

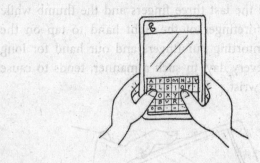

Remedy

- Touch your keypad lightly and don't grip the phone too hard.
- Maintain good posture.

SIMPLE TIPS FOR HEALTHIER SMARTPHONE USE

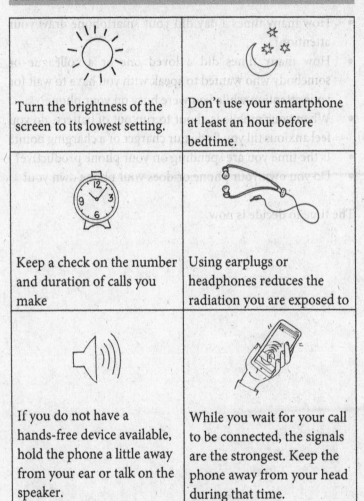

Turn the brightness of the screen to its lowest setting.	Don't use your smartphone at least an hour before bedtime.
Keep a check on the number and duration of calls you make	Using earplugs or headphones reduces the radiation you are exposed to
If you do not have a hands-free device available, hold the phone a little away from your ear or talk on the speaker.	While you wait for your call to be connected, the signals are the strongest. Keep the phone away from your head during that time.

Smartphones have become an inseparable part of our lives, separating us from family, friends and even ourselves. We must introspect on their role in our everyday routine.

Questions to reflect on:

- How many times a day did your smartphone draw your attention?
- How many times did a loved one or a colleague or somebody who wanted to speak with you have to wait for your attention while you were busy on your phone?
- When your mobile is about to run out of battery, do you feel anxious till you find your charger or a charging point?
- Is the time you are spending on your phone productive?
- Do you own your phone or does your phone own you?

The time to decide is now.

15

Digital Wellness

Rishabh was sitting in his living room, talking to his wife about life. They talked about the idea of life and death. He said to his wife, 'Never let me live in a vegetative state, totally dependent on machines, if I am ever hospitalized and am seriously ill. If you see me in that state, I want you to pull the plug; I would much rather die.'

His wife got up from her seat and proceeded to unplug the TV, the computer, the Wi-Fi, the iPod, and the Xbox . . .

Rishabh almost died!

Well, anyone would feel like that if we take their gadgets away. So, if we cannot afford to disconnect from our devices completely, we should at least learn to connect with them better, and use them to our advantage.

Are You Digitally Addicted?

What is the first thing that you do in the morning? Admit it to yourself in all honesty. It has to be looking for your phone or reaching for it to turn off the alarm or checking the time on it, is it not?

Do you check your WhatsApp messages, emails, Facebook, Instagram and Twitter accounts even before you have taken a sip of your morning tea?

Does this happen automatically, despite there being no urgency to do so?

The rest of the day probably follows the same course. Your phone buzzes, signalling the arrival of a new text, and you find yourself unable to resist checking it. You receive a notification that a new email has arrived and you immediately drop everything to read it. You visit Facebook, promising yourself that you'll only spend a few minutes on it, only to surf aimlessly for an hour.

If you relate to the above circumstances, I have bad news. It's likely that you are on your way to becoming addicted to technology. The good news is that you can change and reclaim your life.

SYMPTOMS OF DIGITAL ADDICTION

Here are the most common signs of digital addiction. If you have one or two symptoms, that doesn't mean you have an addiction. But if you experience several on a regular basis, it's time to seek some *digital wellness*.

1. **You automatically reach for your phone every few minutes**
   Checking your phone again and again when you are expecting a very important mail or message is not unusual, but it is worrying if your hand goes to check your phone automatically every few minutes, even when there is no notification.

2. **You become anxious if you don't check your notifications immediately**

   You are having a conversation with a friend and suddenly your phone beeps. You don't know what that notification is for—an email, a message or just an app update. You instantly feel the urge to check your phone in the middle of the conversation. Till the time you don't check it, you feel anxious and cannot stop thinking about it. The longer you take to check, the more anxious you become.

3. **You prefer to be online than be around people**

   Any invitation to join your friends for an outing puts you off. You can spend hours surfing aimlessly but can't hold a conversation for more than ten minutes. The hobbies that once filled you with happiness and excitement are long-forgotten.

4. **You experience withdrawal symptoms if you can't be online**

   Internet addiction is not a myth; it is for real. There are millions of people around the world who experience withdrawal symptoms, not unlike drug addicts, when they're prevented from going online. There are studies to show that users who are online for longer periods feel more depressed than users who are online for short periods.[1]

---

[1] Holly B. Shakya, Nicholas A. Christakis, 'Association of Facebook Use With Compromised Well-Being: A Longitudinal Study', *American Journal of Epidemiology* 185, no.3 (February 2017), pp. 203–211.

Here are some questions that can help you determine if you've had such symptoms too:

- Do you feel irritated when you're unable to be online?
- Do you become defensive when your loved ones complain about your surfing habits?
- Is your unrestrained computer use disturbing your day-to-day life—relationships, study, work?
- Has your social life deteriorated as you spend more time online than among people?

5. **You experience the feeling of euphoria when you log on to social media**
- Do you feel ecstatic when you log in to your account and see the likes on your posts?
- Are you happy checking out hundreds of pictures of a friend's vacation posted online?
- Do you feel a sense of well-being when you log in to various social media accounts?

   If so, then your brain's system is reacting in the same way as that of an addict. Whenever you log in, you feel this sudden surge of happiness or excitement. This is because dopamine, the feel-good hormone, floods your brain's pleasure circuit. This creates a sense of euphoria, very similar to what happens with addictive drugs.

6. **You're unable to keep to your schedules because of technology**
   No matter how many apps you have to manage your time and schedule, it requires diligence and discipline to use

them productively and be punctual. People are frequently late for school, work, appointments and meetings as they are preoccupied with their gadgets, checking the latest news, playing games, watching movies or updating profiles.

7. **You take your phone with you into the bathroom**

Our phones are now everything for us, from diary to photo album to even our newspaper. The times when we would take a magazine or newspaper to the loo are long gone. An article stated that 90 per cent of millennials bring their phones into the bathroom.[2] Do you take your phone even for a thirty-second trip to the washroom, or feel extremely disappointed at forgetting to take it?

8. **You sacrifice sleep to spend more time online**

Adequate sleep is the most essential part of life, but unfortunately it is the most ignored one too. The main casualty of our Internet addiction is our sleep. You are aware that you are well past your bedtime watching videos on YouTube, chatting with your friend on Whatsapp or binge-watching the whole season of an online series, but are still unable to put your phone down.

9. **Your communication and interpersonal skills have taken a hit**

Too much time spent in the virtual world has affected our communication skills and made it more difficult

---

[2] '90% of Millennials Use Their Phones In The Bathroom, Claims Study', Mashable.com, https://in.mashable.com/culture/7875/90-of-millennials-use-their-phones-in-the-bathroom-claims-study

to express ourselves easily. As most of the time we communicate through texting, we tend to avoid eye contact when we meet someone in person. An Internet addict uses the Internet as a form of escapism, minimizing the challenges that accompany social interaction. They may find themselves mumbling to themselves while talking to others. While the online world gives them a cover of anonymity, behind which they express their opinion freely, when it comes to putting their point across in front of others, they look for an escape route.

Ask yourself:

- Are you comfortable presenting your opinion in person freely?
- Do you feel confident speaking to someone you are meeting for the first time?

10. You have faced failure in your previous attempts to quit your online addiction

Habits become addictions when we lose control over them. Even though we are aware of their negative repercussions, we find it difficult to quit. It holds true for other types of addictions as well—drinking, smoking, gambling, etc.—as it does for digital addiction. If you have tried to restrict your Internet time earlier but failed again and again, you are likely an addict. But the good news is that you have accepted that it is a problem and you have a desire to overcome it.

You may check your mobile addiction by going through an online test using the following link:

https://virtual-addiction.com/smartphone-compulsion-test/

ROOT CAUSES OF DIGITAL ADDICTION

Before treating a disease, we should always try to determine the root cause. That will make it easier to resolve it permanently. Let's discuss some of the major root causes of digital addiction:

1. **Societal Expectations**

   Mobile phones, laptops and tablets were considered luxuries till a decade ago. Owners of these gadgets were looked at with envy. But things have changed now. These have become a necessary part of our everyday life. Owning expensive phones has become a norm in our society. This has collectively increased pressure on all of us. We feel compelled to buy the latest model of a phone even if our old one is working fine. We feel ashamed of carrying even one-year-old models and wish to show off the latest ones with aplomb. We buy expensive gadgets for our children just because their friends own them. We are expected to carry our phones and other devices with us, whether we are at home, office or on vacation, because people feel bad if you don't reply to their messages or calls immediately. Not just that, we even feel pressurized to be updated on all the latest happenings, whether it's the news or things that have gone 'viral', just because we want to look informed in our social circle.

Each time we act on these impulses triggered by societal pressure, we are feeding our addiction.

2. Fear of Missing Out (FOMO)
'For a limited period'
'Only few days left'
'Last few items left'

These are some of the lines that call out to us from online ads wherever we look. Discounts are often advertised as available 'only for the weekend'. Products are announced to be available 'in limited quantities'. This is just another way for companies to cash in on our fear of missing out on a gratifying experience. The same applies for messages, emails, voicemails, news, etc. We fear missing out on any of them. We feel compelled to follow these things regularly just because we don't want to miss out on anything. So much so that a message or a call has to be immediately checked or addressed, even when we are driving! Not because there is any emergency, but because of our FOMO. This act of instantly attending to calls and messages soon becomes a habit and then an addiction.

3. Dopamine Rush
The release of dopamine in our brain is the one big reason behind all addictions. Studies have shown that activities such as playing video games, spending time on Facebook, reading text messages and searching for things on Google releases the feel-good hormone, dopamine. Dopamine, a neurotransmitter, provides a sense of pleasure and once you experience this, you want to experience it again

and again. Every time we check a new message from a friend, a new picture posted by a loved one or receive a lot of 'likes' on our posts, we feel the same rush—that's dopamine. This is what makes us addicted to video games, social media and all our gadgets, as their use releases dopamine in our system. Just as a cocaine addict is always on the lookout for their next hit, so is a technology addict.

4. Information Overload

About thirty years ago, we received information in the form of newspapers, magazines and a handful of television programmes. If we needed to research a topic, we visited the library. Today, information comes at us in the form of a flood through our phones, computers and hundreds of TV channels. We further add to this by setting up Google Alerts, subscribing to newsletters, visiting a number of websites and blogs, and spending hours on social media. We're drowning ourselves in this flood of information. This keeps us addicted to technology as we crave for more and more information and entertainment around the clock.

DIGITAL WELLNESS TECHNIQUES

It's high time you make a few changes in your lifestyle to improve your digital wellness. These are actually quite simple but need a strong resolve.

You need to follow a *digital wellness plan* to reduce the stress, anxiety, depression and compulsion that you feel due to the wrong use of technology. It's very similar to fasting. But instead of abstaining from food, you have to abstain from technology. The manner in which people fast varies from person to person. Some people fast on alternate days while others eat after a gap of sixteen hours (intermittent fasting), and yet others fast by eating only one meal a day. The idea is to help your body get rid of toxins that accumulate due to your unhealthy eating habits. Similarly, in digital fasting, you may choose an **'E-Free Day'**, where you don't use your gadgets for a day, or an intermittent fast, where you choose to stay away from technology for a particular number of hours. There may also be 'cheat time' for you to ease into it. You choose the way that suits you best, one that you can follow without feeling too overwhelmed.

Powerful Digital Wellness Mantra

D – Be Diligent and Disciplined
I – Introspect periodically
G – Be Grateful and not greedy
I – Involvement in things outside of yourself
T – Time for yourself, family and friends
A – Ask each time you move your hand to lift mobile
L – Leisure breaks to Laugh and to Live

SEVEN-DAY WELLNESS PLAN

Life was much simpler when Apple and
Blackberry were only fruits.

We bring to you a seven-day wellness plan. Follow these instructions by adding a new instruction each day while following the previous one side by side.

Day 1 – Stop using your phone as an alarm clock

You should not start your day with your phone in hand. If you need something to wake you up in the morning, invest in an alarm clock. It will take away the temptation to browse on your phone and check all the messages and updates as soon as you wake up or when you're still half-asleep. As you know, once you embark on that trip, it will be impossible to turn back unless you have checked everything and probably things you didn't need to either.

Day 2 – Make your bedroom an e-free zone

When we use certain spaces for certain activities, the brain associates that space with those activities. This is called neuro-associative conditioning. If we lie in our bed at night, browsing through our phone and not sleeping, our brain associates the bed with 'not sleeping'. This is how we develop sleep disorders. We watch TV, work on our laptops, surf on our phone on our beds—our brain ends up associating our bed with all these things. You must leave your smartphones, laptop, tablet and other digital devices outside your bedroom when it's time to sleep. This will take away the urge to switch them on. Your bedroom should be e-free, that is, free from any radiation emanating from various electronic gadgets.

Day 3 – Switch off all your notifications

The very nature of alerts and notifications is to draw and manipulate your attention. Once you decline the offer to be notified of each and every message and email, it then becomes an active choice to check them—something that can be controlled more easily. Once you take this step, you will notice a remarkable drop in the number of times your hand reaches your phone automatically.

Day 4 – Do not carry your phone to a meal

In a family where all the members are busy in their routines the whole day, meal times are an opportunity to bond and connect. Constantly checking your phones take away the quality and meaningfulness from the experience of sharing a meal. The dining area should be a sacred space where gadgets are restricted. Parents should lead by example and make sharing a meal a cherished and powerful ritual.

Day 5 – Spend time with your family

This should be done without it being externally enforced, but unfortunately that is not the case. Make a point of spending time with your family without any interruptions from gadgets. You can begin with an hour every day, which may seem a lot initially, but doing this will help strengthen your relationships and mental well-being.

Day 6 – Plan your screen time wisely

If your day begins and ends with looking at an inanimate six-inch screen, completely refraining from doing that may sound like a death knell to you. So, opt for the other alternatives: try and schedule your screen time. You may plan to check your phone only during particular time slots in the day, such as for fifteen minutes starting at 10 a.m., 2 p.m. and 6 p.m.; you can come up with your own slots according to your schedule. Don't forget to set a time limit.

Also remember, it is always a good idea to read a book instead of using your phone before going to bed as it will not interfere with the quality of your sleep. The blue glare from the phone or laptop screen has been shown to impact melatonin secretion, the hormone that helps you fall asleep, as mentioned before.[3] But, when you read a book, this problem won't arise.

Day 7 – Celebrate a screen-free day

This should be done at least once a week. One full day to remain not just e-free but screen-free. No screens whatsoever—mobiles, tablets, touch devices, TV, etc. For that day, you should make plans with your friends or relatives, or find meaningful and rewarding hobbies that do not involve a digital device. Inform your family, friends and colleagues about your e-free day in advance. This will save them from worrying if you do not reply to any calls and messages. And once you have already announced your commitment to the world, it will motivate you to keep to it.

These small and moderate changes will surely help you connect with the important things in your life that you have been unknowingly sacrificing while spending all your time staring at your screen.

---

[3] G. Tosini, I. Ferguson, K. Tsubota, 'Effects of Blue Light on the Circadian System and Eye Physiology', *Molecular Vision*, no.22 (2016), pp. 61-72.

THE BRAIN TRANSFORMS ITSELF

As discussed in Chapter 4, whenever you want to adopt any new practice in your life, your brain will start helping you do that more effectively by growing new connections and new neurons because of its wonderful characteristic called *neuroplasticity*. This needs to be remembered while practising digital wellness too.

- Within just one week of *practice*, the brain will start sprouting neurons, which will help to make new connections to record your new learning in your brain.
- Within eight weeks of *practice*, your brain will physically change, to help you continue with the positive practice.
- New positive habits can be created with *practice* over a period of time.
- Digital wellness techniques can be *practised* regularly for the greatest benefits.

Practice is the key word in all the above points because that's what the brain seems to love. Whatever you keep practising, the brain will make easier and easier for you to do the next time.

You need to feel inspired and optimistic about your digital wellness; it should be something that you actively want to do, rather than something that you feel you are compelled to do. Only then will you see the results that will transform your life for the better.

16

Multitasking Is a Myth

Having breakfast while getting ready for work, speaking on the phone while checking emails, speaking on the phone while driving, studying for an exam and keeping one eye on the cricket match score, watching TV and texting a friend at the same time. Does this sound familiar? Is this something you do often?

Most of us live by the conviction that multitasking is something indispensable for us to survive in these fast-paced modern times. We don't just cook anymore—we follow recipes online, cook, text, talk on the phone and upload photos of the meal we just made or are in the process of making, simultaneously.

Multitasking has also become an essential skill during the process of recruitment at firms. All employees are expected to be good multitaskers. Employers believe that with so many different tasks and hurried deadlines, the employees have to be prepared to handle multiple things at once.

As a result, all of us keep trying to master the art of doing more than one thing at a time. We feel the pressure to move faster and faster and to do more and more to keep up with our competitive existence—no wonder it is called 'the grind'. We often live under the illusion that multitasking is a skill that will teach us time management and improve our ability to meet deadlines. But is that true?

People are proud of their multitasking skills, but the truth is that multitasking is as illusionary as it is inefficient. It should not be something to brag about. In fact, the whole idea of **multitasking is a myth.** The truth in almost 99 per cent cases is that people are just doing rapid *task-switching* and ultimately hampering their own focus and productivity. Multiple studies have confirmed that the human brain cannot perform two tasks that require high-level brain function at the same time.[1] This of course does not include helping execute low-level, routine bodily functions like breathing and pumping blood. Only the tasks you have to 'think' about are considered high-level. What actually happens when you think you are multitasking is that **you are rapidly switching between tasks.**

THE HUMAN BRAIN JUST CAN'T MULTITASK

Multitasking is scientifically impossible, because that simply isn't how our brains are designed to work. Our prefrontal cortex is the control centre of the brain, which regulates our focus. Linked to both the halves of the brain, the prefrontal cortex coordinates with other areas of the brain that are necessary for maintaining attention and achieving set goals.

---

[1] H. Pashler, 'Dual-Task Interference in Simple Tasks: Data and Theory', *Psychological Bulletin 116*, no.2 (1994), pp. 220–244.

With the massive amount of computing power in our brain, it is natural to assume that the cortex can independently handle two tasks, but that isn't the case. When you attempt to tackle more than one task, it may seem like you are focusing on two, three or four things at once, but in fact, the brain is just shifting focus very rapidly. For a healthy brain, this shift can happen almost instantaneously, leading people to believe that they are juggling numerous tasks successfully, when in fact people's brains are just changing their focal points in a matter of milliseconds, and not concentrating well on each task.

Let's consider a simple everyday situation where one may have to 'multitask' and see closely what happens:

- Dhruv was at his desk in office, replying to an email. The task had his complete attention. Just then his colleague came to interrupt him and asked if Dhruv had the time to answer a question. *Switch*.
- He tried for a few seconds to keep typing the email while his colleague spoke, but then stopped typing and turned to listen to him. *Switch*.
- Dhruv was trying to pay attention to what his colleague was saying, but at the back of his mind, he wanted to get back to the email. *Switch*.
- Dhruv asked his colleague to repeat what he was saying once he was finally ready to pay full attention. *Switch*.
- After listening to the question, Dhruv gave a hurried answer and turned his attention back to the computer. *Switch*.
- Because of the break in concentration, Dhruv had to reorient himself with what he had been typing. He tried

to retrace the lost train of thoughts. It took some time to figure out, but finally he got back to work.

Dhruv really wasn't doing two things at one time, was he? He was merely *task-switching*. He switched back and forth between two tasks so fast that he didn't realize it. It seemed as though he was handling two things at a time, but he was actually jumping mental tracks during that whole exchange. So, was it really multitasking or merely **task-switching**? We can judge for ourselves.

Let's do an exercise to understand this further:

	MULTITASKING IS WORSE THAN A LIE
1.	
2.	
3.	
4.	

Round 1

1. Set your stopwatch to time your activity or have someone time you.
2. In the first row in the table above, you have to write the sentence 'Multitasking is worse than a lie'. However, for every letter you write, you need to immediately write its count just below it in the next row (row number 2). For example, after writing **M** in the first row, write **1** in the second row. Next write **U** in the first row and **2** in the second row, and so on. Just make sure that you write one number after every letter in the sentence.

3. Note the time taken to complete the above task, i.e. to write the sentence and the numbers in rows 1 and 2 respectively.
4. After completing this round, you will have the sentence 'Multitasking is worse than a lie' written in the first row and the numbers 1 to 27 in the second row.

Round 2

1. Reset your stopwatch.
2. In the third row, copy the entire sentence 'Multitasking is worse than a lie' in one go.
3. After writing the complete sentence, switch to the fourth row and write the numbers from 1 to 27.
4. Note the time taken to complete this round.
5. At the end of this round, you will have the sentence 'Multitasking is worse than a lie' written in the third row and the numbers 1 to 27 in the fourth row.

Now, compare the time taken to complete both the rounds. Typically, a person task-switching in Round 1 compared with focusing on one task at a time in Round 2

- takes **more time** to complete the exercise.
- can see a considerable **decrease in the quality of work**. There might be mistakes in spellings or numbering.
- is bound to experience **more cognitive stress.**

What we did in Round 1 is pretty much the same as what we believe to be multitasking. We were attempting to do two things at the same time. Every time we switched back and forth between the letters and the numbers, there was a cost to pay. The movement of the pen was costing us a little more time to complete the task. And moreover, every time we went back and forth we had to remember where we were—it required more mental effort.

People believe doing more than one task together saves time, but it is not so. It is actually very costly. It is a less effective and less efficient way to get things done.

Multitasking   Task-switching

MULTITASKING MULTIPLIES TENSION AND DIVIDES ATTENTION

Recent studies by researchers at University of California, San Francisco, and University of Michigan show that multitasking, or rather task-switching, among reading emails, surfing the web and checking up on friends' Facebook posts, etc., could have a draining effect on the brain's ability to rest and to think deeply on a particular subject. [2]

---

[2] 'Multitasking: Switching Costs', American Psychological Association, 20 March 2006, https://www.apa.org/research/action/multitask

- **Multitasking reduces your IQ and EQ**
  Neuroscientists from the UK have examined physical changes in the brains of some children (test subjects) who were found to have been prone to rapid task-switching between multimedia devices, such as using smartphones while watching television or texting while playing video games on the computer, etc. These kids were later diagnosed with significant damages in the part of the brain that deals with primary senses and expression of emotions, empathy, etc. Unfortunately, the primary damage was deemed capable of even deeper mental damage with prolonged task-switching.

Neuroscientists at the Institute of Cognitive Neuroscience at University College, London, scanned the brains of people who frequently multitask. They discovered that these people 'had smaller gray matter density in the anterior cingulate cortex', which is responsible for empathy as well as cognitive and emotional control. The scientists 'observed decreased cognitive control performance'. The participants experienced decline in their IQ score which was similar to people who had smoked marijuana or stayed up all night. IQ drops of 15 points for multitasking men lowered their scores to the average range of an eight-year-old child. Multitasking in meetings and other social situations shows low self- and social-awareness, which are the two important emotional skills to succeed at work.[3]

---

[3] Travis Bradberry, 'Multitasking Damages Your Brain and Your Career, New Studies Suggest', Talentsmart.com, https://www.talentsmart.com/articles/Multitasking-Damages-Your-Brain-and-Your-Career,-New-Studies-Suggest-2102500909-p-1.html

- **It reduces mental performance and efficiency**
Whenever we create a thought in our mind, we are actually using up energy. Frequent shifting of our thoughts from one task to another drains precious brain resources and energy. Multitasking reduces productivity and increases the chance of errors.

- **It kills creativity**
Creative work, such as sculpting, painting, making music, writing stories or poems, etc., needs longer attention spans. If we are involved in more than one task at a time, we will not be able to hold our attention on it for a long time, which can kill creativity. For example, when I [Aditi] write a chapter of a book, I keep all my gadgets out of my room as even a small distraction disrupts my thought process. My full concentration is then on the content that I am planning to write. Although I can do the same work while doing another task, like listening to music or answering door bells, but the quality of my creative endeavour shall suffer greatly due to constant task-switching. When there is a well-defined practical task, it is relatively easier to concentrate even in a noisy environment, but a creative endeavour demands an environment that encourages reflection and introspection. It is almost meditative in its nature. Therefore, it is important to keep it isolated from all types of distractions, because you are creating something new at the moment.

- **It leads to stress**
Everyone today is juggling too many things at a time, and when demand exceeds ability, it leads to stress. Multitasking increases production of cortisol, also known

as the stress hormone. A constant flow of stress hormones strains the body and threatens physical as well as mental health.

- **Multitasking is addictive**
  When we complete a task, no matter how small it is, our brain produces dopamine. It rewards us for completing tasks and motivates us to repeat them. We keep trying to do multiple tasks together to get one dopamine hit after the other. Even the tasks that do not require any critical thinking (like sending a mail, checking updates on social networking sites, posting pictures online, etc.) make us feel that we have achieved a lot, and it turns to neural addiction. When we do not have much to do, we miss that feeling of gratification and think that we are wasting our time focusing only on one task.

WHY IS MULTITASKING GIVEN SO MUCH IMPORTANCE?

Multitasking was originally never meant to define the way humans operate. It was initially coined as a computing term.

'In computing, multitasking is the concurrent execution of multiple tasks (also known as processes) over a certain period of time. New tasks can interrupt already started ones before they finish, instead of waiting for them to end. As a result, a computer executes segments of multiple tasks in an *interleaved manner*, while the tasks share common processing resources such as central processing units (CPUs) and main memory.'[4]

---

4 'Computer Multitasking', Wikipedia, https://en.wikipedia.org/wiki/Computer_multitasking

With time, we came to describe our increasingly hectic world in computing terms and compare the human brain with computers. It soon became a popular trend to use this term for humans as well to indicate their increased machine-like capabilities and efficiency. But when most people talk about multitasking, they are really talking about task-switching.

Saying that you're a good multitasker is the same as saying that you're good at using a less effective method to get things done. No matter how effective you are at switching among tasks, you are still working less efficiently than you can. You are going to take longer to get things done than the person who focuses on one activity at a time.

When we multitask (rather switch-task) while interacting with other human beings, the switching cost is higher than just the time involved. The people we live with and work with on a daily basis deserve our full attention. When we give people divided attention, we end up damaging relationships.

You might feel that there are some tasks that you are able to do very well simultaneously, such as listening to your favourite songs while driving. So why doesn't this lead to stress?

The right term for such tasks is not multitasking, but **background tasking.**

Background tasking is when you perform two or more tasks where only one of those tasks requires mental effort. Other examples of background tasking could be eating dinner and watching TV, or jogging and listening to music. Working on your computer while you wait for the printer to print pages is another perfect example of background tasking.

Task switching, on the other hand, is always less efficient and less effective. Background tasking has the potential to be efficient and effective if it is used properly. But for achieving the best levels of concentration, the mantra is **Monotasking**. It is the process by which you focus on well-timed execution and completion of an individual task and then commence the next task. This sequential uptake of tasks is less exhausting and enables us to retain focus on each task.

MYTHS ABOUT MULTITASKING

MYTH	REALITY
Multitasking (or task-switching) saves time and thus is the best form of time management.	Monotasking is the best form of time management while 'task-switching' only adds to inefficiency and mental stress.
Multitasking is a trait best suited for talented professionals.	Professionals are the victims of multitasking.
Multitasking does not adversely affect one's concentration.	Deficit in concentration and attention is a result of multitasking.
Men find it difficult to multitask, but for women, it's a way of life.	There is a lack of evidence demonstrating a gender difference when we talk about multitasking.
Multitasking has no ill-effects and is not addictive.	Multitasking or task-switching in excess is very harmful for productivity, mental well-being and is in fact quite addictive.

HOW TO AVOID MULTITASKING

Life is not going to slow down for anyone. Multitasking is essentially bad, as deduced in this chapter. So how are we going to cope? Won't we be left behind if we don't multitask?

No, we are going to match pace with this ultra-busy life and that too without multitasking or task-switching.

Here is a *mantra* that will make it possible. All you have to do is: **MONOTASK**

M – Meditation. When you find yourself in the middle of a storm of tasks and responsibilities, take a minute to meditate. A calm state of mind will help you to look at your work more objectively. Regular meditation helps you to maintain your sanity even in the toughest and busiest of times.

O – One task at a time. No matter how compelled you feel to handle more than a task at a time, be determined to take up only one task at a time. It will give you the best results as it will be the only thing you'll be concentrating on.

N – Learn to say 'no' to distractions. No social media, no emails, no messages, no calls while doing important work. Say 'no' to less important work. Delegate things that can be delegated. Don't take on extra work just to please others. Say 'no' to negative thoughts that may take away your confidence. A simple two-letter word can reduce most of your burden.

O – Organize. Clutter outside creates clutter inside. A more organized workplace or home will also bring clarity of thoughts in our life. This will help a great deal in improving concentration. The better our concentration on our task, the less time we will take to finish it.

T – Techno-Smart. Advancements in technology are making our life simpler every day. It is up to us to make the best use of it. Stay updated about the latest gadgets, tools, apps and software, so you can use them to complete your tasks in the least possible time with the best possible results.

A – Acceptance. Accept that multitasking is not as beneficial as it is assumed to be. No matter how tempting it is to handle two or three tasks at a time and be done with your to-do list at the earliest, it is better to do one task at a time with full concentration. Monotasking is the best way of saving time and getting your task done in the best possible manner.

S – Scheduling. Making a daily or a weekly schedule of the work that you have to accomplish is half your task done. It helps you prioritize the tasks and demarcate your timelines. It gives a clearer picture of what you have to accomplish and in what duration. Time thus saved is energy saved.

K – Kill Procrastination. Procrastination is your biggest enemy. Delaying a task results in piling up of work, and you are forced to multitask. It leads to stress, anxiety, unfinished tasks and poor quality of work. Even if the deadline of a given assignment is a week away, do it now. It will take away your stress and leave enough time to handle unexpected tasks that may come later. Remember: The right time to do an important task is 'Now'.

> *'The shorter way to do many things is to only do one thing at a time.'*
>
> **Mozart**

17

One-Minute Activities
for Improving Concentration

Activity 1

In the given activity, cross out (X) and count as many b's as possible in one minute.

bddbddbbdbbdbdbdbd
bddbddbbdbbdbdbdbd
dbdbdbdbbdbbbbbbbb
bddbbbdbbdbdbdbdb
bddbdbdbbdbbbbbbbb
ddbdbbdbdbbdbdbdbd
dbdbdbdbbdbbbbbbbb
bbdbbbddbbdbdbdbdb
dbdbdbdbbdbbbbbbbb
bdbdbbdbdbbdbdbdbd
bddbdbdbbdbbbbbbbb
ddbdbbdbdbbdbdbdbd

Total number of b's you crossed =

ACTIVITY 2

In the given activity, cross out (X) and count as many q's as possible in one minute.

```
qpqpqqppqqpqqpqpqp
qqppqqpqpqqppppppp
qppqpqpqpqpqpqpqp
pqpqpqppqqpqqpqpqq
qpqpqqpqqpqqpqpqpq
pqqpqqppqqpppqpqpq
qqppqppqpqqpqqqqqq
pqpqpqpqpqpqppppp
qpppqqppqqqppppppp
qpqpqqpqqppppqpqpq
pqpqpqpqpqpqppppp
qpppqqppqqqppppppp
pqpqpqpqpqpqppppp
qpppqqppqqqppppppp
pqpqpqpqpqpqppppp
qpppqqppqqqppppppp
pqpqpqpqpqpqpppppp
qpppqqppqqqppppppp
pqpqpqpqpqpqpppppp
qpppqqppqqqppppppp
pqpqpqpqpqpqpppppp
qpppqqppqqqppppppp
pqpqpqpqpqpqpppppp
qpppqqppqqqppppppp
```

Total number of q's you crossed =

ACTIVITY 3

In the given activity, cross out (X) and count as many L's as
possible in one minute.

```
L T T L T T L L T T L T T L T L T L
T T L L T T L T L T T L L L L L L L
T L L T L T L T L T L L T L T L T L
T L L T T L L T T L T T L T L T L T
T L T L T T L T T L T T L T L T L T
L T T L T T L L T T L L L T L T L T
T T L L T L L T L T T L T T T T T T
L T L T L T L T L T L T L L L L L L
T L L L T T L L T T T L L L L L L L
T L T L T T L T T L L L L T L T L T
L T L T L T L T L T L T L L L L L L
T L L L T T L L T T T L L L L L L L
L T L T L T L T L T L T L L L L L L
T L L L T T L L T T T L L L L L L L
T L T L T T L T T L L L L T L T L T
L T L T L T L T L T L T L L L L L L
T L L L T T L L T T T L L L L L L L
L T L T L T L T L T L T L L L L L L
T L L L T T L L T T T L L L L L L L
T L T L T T L T T L L L L T L T L T
L T L T L T L T L T L T L L L L L L
T L L L T T L L T T T L L L L L L L
L T L T L T L T L T L T L L L L L L
```

Total number of L's you crossed =

ACTIVITY 4

In the given activity, cross out (X) and count as many M's as possible in one minute.

```
M W W M W W M M W M M W M W M W M W W
M W W M W W M M W M M W M W M W M W M W
W M W M W M W M M W M M M M M M M M
M W W M M M W W M M W M W M W M W M
M W W M W M W M M W M M M M M M M M
W W M W M M W M W M M W M W M W M W W
W M W M W M W M M W M M M M M M M M
M M W M M M M W W M M W M W M W M W M
W M W M W M W M M W M M M M M M M M
M W M W M M W M W M M W M W M W M W W
M W W M W M W M M W M M M M M M M M
W W M W M M W M W M M W M W M W M W W
M M W M M M M W W M M W M W M W M W M
W M W M W M W M M W M M M M M M M M
M W M W M M W M W M M W M W M W M W W
M W W M W M W M M W M M M M M M M M
W W M W M M W M W M M W M W M W M W W
M M W M M M W W M M W M W M W M W M
W M W M W M W M M W M M M M M M M M
M W M W M M W M W M M W M W M W M W W
M W W M W M W M M W M M M M M M M M
W W M W M M W M W M M W M W M W M W W
M W W M W M W M M W M M M M M M M M
```

Total number of M's you crossed =

ACTIVITY 5

In the given activity, cross out (X) and count as many 9's as possible in one minute.

```
6996996669669696969
6996996669669696969
9696969669669696666
6996669966696969696
6996969669669696666
9969669696669696969
9696969669669666666
6696669966696969696
9696969669669666666
6969669696669696969
6996969669669696666
9969669696669696969
6696669966696969696
9696969669669666666
6969669696669696969
6996969669669696666
9969669696669696969
6696669966696969696
9696969669669666666
6969669696669696969
6996969669669696666
9969669696669696969
6696669966696969696
```

Total number of 9's you crossed =

ACTIVITY 6

Try to connect box A with A; B with B; and C with C, but without any of the lines crossing each other.

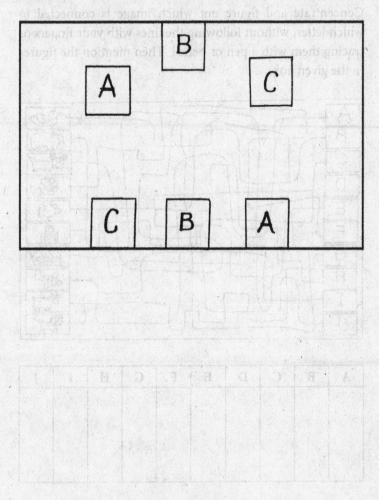

ACTIVITY 7

The lines in the figure below begin from the letters on the left side and are connected to some images on the right side. Concentrate and figure out which image is connected to which letter, without following the lines with your fingers or tracing them with a pen or pencil. Then mention the figures in the given box.

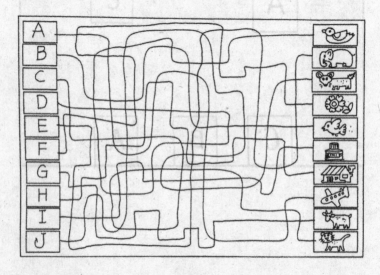

A	B	C	D	E	F	G	H	I	J

Some more fun exercises for you:

1. **Count backwards from 100 to 1**
    This may sound simple enough, and it is. However, it takes a bit of concentration to do it.

2. **Spell words backwards**
    This is great for kids and can be enjoyed with other family members as well. It has the added bonus of helping the young ones learn spellings.

3. **Count common words in a paragraph in a newspaper, book or magazine.**
    Find words like 'it' or 'and' or 'the' without using a finger to spot them.

4. **Do some simple mathematical calculations in your mind**
    This is a very good exercise to improve concentration.

Solution

ACTIVITY 6

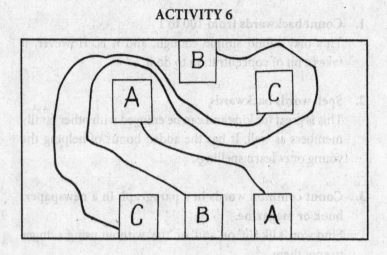

18

Concentration Grids

Here are a few concentration grids to help you concentrate better and increase your attention span.

- Start your timer.
- Begin marking numbers starting from 0 to 99 in a sequence.
- You can circle them (O) or strike them off (×).
- Stop your timer as soon as you reach the number 99 and record the time taken by you.
- Try another grid and compare the time taken.

Another way to do this exercise is to see how many numbers you can find in a set time limit.

For example, set the timer to 45 seconds or a minute, and see which number you reach at in that much time. Try with the same time slot again and see how much further you can go.

Record the result of each attempt and track your improvement.

GRID 1

20	68	87	80	15	83	36	72	48	90
74	82	26	37	65	14	73	12	99	16
24	70	58	52	46	91	41	50	79	03
81	84	85	06	22	38	27	18	08	23
89	86	66	31	92	42	62	64	13	59
32	21	30	04	10	60	98	39	47	75
63	51	35	28	95	67	00	09	01	76
78	55	54	07	71	96	49	93	77	69
53	45	17	05	33	44	61	43	19	88
56	02	34	94	40	97	11	29	57	25

Time taken: _____

GRID 2

92	48	60	77	90	17	14	42	78	66
57	79	72	64	26	96	01	32	81	68
46	20	76	38	18	88	82	13	54	11
29	89	23	03	27	49	86	75	74	24
09	83	70	47	56	43	45	33	40	41
94	22	61	80	98	67	21	25	15	93
36	87	05	28	44	91	51	02	08	73
71	34	55	95	58	85	07	10	35	31
59	19	39	04	62	50	52	00	96	37
16	12	30	97	65	99	06	84	53	63

Time taken: _____

GRID 3

52	13	21	73	39	07	35	82	58	31
65	42	59	98	96	97	24	63	71	06
38	81	85	18	27	70	89	76	25	60
09	75	90	57	99	10	84	91	48	36
17	26	01	43	00	74	12	69	41	08
62	47	92	37	88	14	56	32	53	22
72	05	66	46	77	68	45	04	61	49
28	86	11	15	34	87	93	80	64	51
50	83	94	55	95	54	29	33	16	19
67	79	30	02	40	23	78	03	20	44

Time taken: _____

GRID 4

29	44	08	79	30	17	39	26	15	63
35	59	41	20	22	83	92	56	65	33
01	16	73	48	95	87	96	77	70	03
51	10	81	99	98	94	82	86	45	13
07	67	53	04	40	05	62	49	75	52
60	38	85	93	69	97	28	24	02	61
25	46	76	55	34	64	89	90	36	42
68	32	91	88	84	37	12	71	00	11
47	18	57	27	43	54	74	80	72	66
14	06	78	31	23	58	19	09	50	21

Time taken: _____

GRID 5

30	66	91	38	68	44	47	81	21	10
11	02	84	73	36	57	46	13	64	61
52	62	71	09	80	60	92	88	42	94
33	95	15	31	69	16	14	07	06	82
12	28	17	55	96	58	04	05	48	72
23	67	89	79	26	22	59	49	70	76
54	85	56	18	99	20	63	83	93	24
50	41	27	19	51	75	65	77	53	40
32	39	98	74	43	86	34	29	90	01
08	87	45	97	37	35	00	25	78	03

Time taken: _____

GRID 6

21	83	95	04	79	16	28	96	76	49
50	42	99	39	86	84	57	69	77	26
00	25	87	08	19	90	91	92	30	62
37	59	93	09	43	13	85	53	88	36
68	32	56	41	97	46	47	27	78	10
81	72	02	33	82	64	23	61	74	73
35	34	48	18	45	15	51	94	07	03
20	66	55	89	60	58	31	70	80	06
52	14	72	54	40	24	98	29	17	44
01	71	22	63	05	12	38	67	11	65

Time taken: _____

GRID 7

33	57	48	17	25	64	87	60	46	30
63	07	75	67	98	54	92	73	05	18
11	27	95	93	21	99	14	81	26	53
70	78	82	04	43	96	51	90	71	40
41	19	89	84	34	38	94	37	76	49
61	66	01	50	79	03	10	15	65	08
09	74	91	02	88	77	25	56	42	22
44	31	86	97	69	59	35	85	06	12
23	52	80	29	62	13	83	24	20	32
47	16	36	72	39	55	68	45	58	00

Time taken: _____

GRID 8

55	71	99	17	13	24	00	18	84	70
86	36	92	22	45	26	81	04	42	69
58	76	80	16	96	66	57	63	43	61
19	39	21	53	87	74	25	67	85	89
79	32	09	29	93	05	97	14	47	46
91	23	94	20	68	41	33	59	35	03
95	37	54	38	62	82	49	90	75	65
40	88	31	07	53	02	12	01	50	28
34	72	60	11	51	83	27	56	06	08
98	73	77	15	78	64	10	44	30	48

Time taken: _____

GRID 9

20	29	06	65	19	54	73	36	72	43
45	61	23	77	86	03	99	90	13	51
39	82	57	21	26	44	97	00	27	34
50	04	63	89	52	15	33	85	94	17
55	12	84	01	35	68	98	92	81	69
31	49	25	71	41	48	78	95	11	47
10	46	91	83	62	58	70	37	87	40
16	74	14	38	08	96	53	67	30	09
22	42	66	79	59	28	75	05	24	56
02	64	18	76	93	80	88	60	32	07

Time taken: _____

GRID 10

62	28	11	96	26	71	22	12	70	63
36	50	00	61	99	59	01	80	67	47
64	68	53	17	21	79	05	49	08	04
48	66	56	15	55	44	32	20	16	35
29	76	51	23	81	46	65	75	93	57
43	03	82	90	33	45	86	87	73	27
98	31	10	74	30	72	41	06	42	88
18	60	38	77	58	07	24	84	79	19
91	89	95	13	25	09	69	97	94	52
83	39	85	37	40	34	54	02	92	14

Time taken: _____

19

Spot the Differences

Here are some 'spot the differences' activities, to help you concentrate better and increase your attention.

ACTIVITY 1

Spot and circle **ten** differences in the images below:

Image 1 (a)

Image 1 (b)

ACTIVITY 2

Spot and circle **ten** differences in the images below:

Image 2 (a)

Image 2 (b)

ACTIVITY 3

Spot and circle **ten** differences in the images below:

Image 3 (a)

Image 3 (b)

ACTIVITY 4

Spot and circle **ten** differences in the images below:

Image 4 (a)

Image 4 (b)

ACTIVITY 5

Spot and circle **ten** differences in the images below:

Image 5 (a)

Image 5 (b)

Solutions

ACTIVITY 1

ACTIVITY 2

ACTIVITY 3

ACTIVITY 4

ACTIVITY 5

20

Concentration Games

Ball in the Cup Game

Here is a DIY project to make a conventional Indian game. It is an effective way to make your mind and body active. You'll use hand-eye coordination and be fully present in the moment and on the job at hand, which will help you develop your concentration skills.

You will need:

- A polystyrene or plastic cup
- A string
- A ping-pong ball
- A sharpened pencil

How to Make It

1. Punch a small hole in the centre of the bottom of the cup with a sharp pencil.

191

2. Tie several knots at the end of a 50 cm long string. Thread the string through the hole in the cup from the inside to the outside so that the knots are held in place at the bottom.

3. Punch a small hole in a ping pong ball with the sharp pencil.

4. Tie several knots at the other end of the 50 cm string. Using the pencil, gently push the knotted end of the string through the hole in the ping-pong ball.

5. Hold the cup in one hand. Thrust the ball in the air and try to catch it in the cup as it falls back down. If you practise without tying the ball to the cup, it'll fall on the floor repeatedly and may break your concentration.

Bouncing Game

Take a bouncy ball and bounce it off the floor. Concentrate so that you continue to bounce it for as long as possible. Compete with your friends or family members and have them count how many times you are able to bounce it, which will help both you and them improve concentration skills! Here is a table to keep track of your scores.

Record:

Name of the player	No. of bounces	Name of the player	No. of bounces	Name of the player	No. of bounces

21

Yoga and Pranayam
to Improve Concentration

The scattered or distracted condition of the mind is a quality generally referred to as being *Chanchala*. The opposite of chanchala is *Ekagra* (*Eka*—one, *Agra*—pointed). In order to harness the power of the mind, one needs to learn to focus it. To make the mind focused—one-pointed—it demands committed dedication. The state of *ekagrata* (where one is ekagra) can be elaborated as a state where the many thoughts in the mind are all related to or *pointed to only one object of focus.*

Indian Yogic system is a pioneer in this specific area of focusing the mind. In a state of ekagrata, the mind becomes still and there is no disturbance; it is completely focused on the object of interest. *Dharana* (focus), *Dhyana* (continued focus) and *Samadhi* (merger, experience of oneness with the object) are three phases of ekagrata according to the Yogic system. You start with focusing on the object of interest, increase the amount of time that you can focus on that object (extended focus) and then you focus completely on the object (only thoughts related to the object arise in the mind)—that is the state of absolute concentration or ekagrata. The 'object' can be physical (a thing) or mental (an idea).

Yogasanas practised all over the world were invented by Indian Yogis to help *control and strengthen the body* so that the body does not disturb the *stillness of the mind* during meditation. In this chapter, we will talk of different ways to make your mind more ekagra.

GYAN MUDRA

When we bring our fingers together in a specific pattern, it stimulates a specific part of the brain. These patterns in which we hold our fingers together are called *mudras* or *yog mudras*. Each of the five fingers regulates a different element in the body as listed below.

Thumb – Fire
Index finger – Air
Middle finger – Space
Ring finger – Earth
Little finger – Water

Out of the twelve common yog mudras, **Gyan mudra** is considered one of the most important mudras for improving memory, concentration and the nervous system. It is also known as 'Knowledge mudra', 'Dhyana mudra' or '*Vayu-vardhak* (one that increases the air element) mudra'. It helps prevent headaches, loss of sleep, tension, anxiety, depression and fears.

How to Do It

1) Sit comfortably with your back and neck straight.

2) Touch the tip of your index finger to the tip of your thumb and keep the rest of the three fingers straight, as shown in the image above. Place your hand on your folded knee, keeping your palm facing up, as shown in the image below.

3) Put a little pressure on the tips of the fingers that are joined. Make sure the rest of the hand is kept straight.

4) You can chant a mantra of your choice in tandem with your breath or simply chant 'Om' as you exhale for a harmonizing effect. Practising this for ten minutes every day will help improve your concentration.

PRANAYAMA

Breathing is a vital involuntary function of our body. *Pranayama is a yoga practice* of controlling the breath to reduce stress and improve physical and mental health.

Here are the instructions on three pranayama exercises that are most beneficial in improving concentration.

1. Nadi Shodhan or Anulom Vilom

This is also known as alternate nostril breathing. It calms the mind, and helps concentrate and remove free radicals and toxins from the body. At the same time, it helps to calm the nervous system.

How to Do It

1) Close your right nostril by pressing it with your thumb.
2) Slowly exhale through the left.
3) Continuing to hold the right nostril closed, inhale through the left as calmly and deeply as possible.

4) Release the right nostril and close the left nostril with your ring finger. Now exhale slowly and deeply through the right.

5) When you have finished exhaling, take a deep breath through the right nostril.

6) Then close the right nostril by pressing it with your thumb and exhale through the left.

7) An inhalation and exhalation through both nostrils completes one cycle.

8) Continue until you have finished three cycles.

9) Then lower your hand and breathe freely through both nostrils.

2. Bhramari Pranayama

This pranayama is an effective way to instantly calm your mind. It is one of the best breathing exercises to release anger, agitation, frustration and anxiety from your mind. *Bhramari* is the name given to the black Indian bee. The exhalation in this pranayama resembles the typical humming sound of a bee, which is how it gets its name.

How to Do It

1) Sit up straight with your eyes closed.
2) Observe the sensations in your body. Place your index fingers on the cartilage between your cheek and ear.

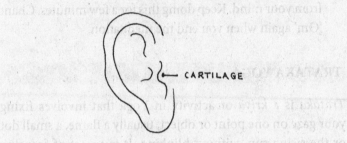

3) Take a deep breath in, and as you breathe out, gently press the cartilage.
4) While keeping the cartilage pressed, make a loud humming sound like a bee.
5) Breathe in again and repeat the exercise. Continue to do it three or four times.

Bhramari Pranayam should be done only in the morning. It should not be done during late afternoon or evening.

3. Omkar

Omkar helps in relaxing our body and makes us feel revitalized. It increases concentration power with continuous practice.

How to Do It

1. Close your eyes. Start by exhaling forcefully, and then breathe in till you feel your stomach is full.

2. Start saying 'Om' for the first few seconds and then end the chanting by transitioning from 'Om' to 'Mmmm'. Make sure this transition is smooth.
3. Once you have completed chanting 'Om', focus on your breath with your eyes closed and try to dispel all thoughts from your mind. Keep doing this for a few minutes. Chant 'Om' again when you end the meditation.

TRATAKA YOGA

Trataka is a *kriya* or activity in Yoga that involves fixing your gaze on one point or object, usually a flame, a small dot or the rising sun, without blinking. It is an act of focusing the eyes and then the mind on one point, to dispel all other thoughts.

Every second, our mind gets flooded with various thoughts, and it becomes difficult for us to concentrate. When we practise Trataka and focus our eyes on a single object or point, it decreases the movement of the eyeballs. This helps us to steady and focus our mind by minimizing the visual stimuli to the very least. This in turn decreases the number of stray thoughts and helps calm the mind.

Trataka can also help to counter and reverse short-sightedness or myopia, as this practice helps to strengthen the eye muscles.

The object of gazing can be a Shiva lingam, flame of a candle, any small dot on the wall, a crystal ball, or even the picture of a deity. Gazing at a candle flame is the most commonly used method to practise this.

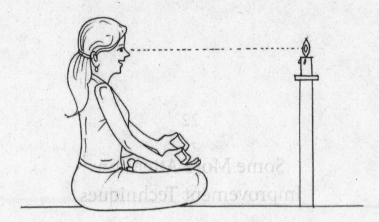

How to Do It

1. Sit on a chair or on the floor with a straight back. If you are sitting on the floor, the cross-legged lotus position of the *padmasana* is the best posture.
2. Light a candle and place it one and a half feet away from you.
3. Place the candle a little below eye level, otherwise it will strain your neck.
4. Look at the portion of the flame just above the wick, as this part of the flame will be steadier.
5. Try to look at the flame without blinking. As you go on practising, it will become easier. You will soon notice only the flame and begin to feel one with it.
6. When the eyes get tired, slowly close them and relax. Your eyes may water too. But you may continue staring at the image for a few more seconds.
7. Slowly open the eyes. Blink a few times to relieve any strain.
8. Repeat this process a few times.

22

Some More Attention Improvement Techniques

Deep Breathing Exercise

Sit comfortably in a chair with a straight back and feet firmly on the ground. Keep your hands on your thighs. Close your eyes and breathe normally. Next, take a deep, slow breath through your nose. Let your stomach expand fully when you breathe in. Now breathe out slowly through your mouth and notice your stomach contract when you breathe out. Your mind might wander to other thoughts. Acknowledge these thoughts, mentally keep them aside, and gently bring your attention back to your breathing. Feel your mind and body relaxing. Try to practise this once or twice a day, always at the same time, mainly to form a habit. Do it for ten or twelve minutes for each cycle.

When we are anxious, our mind **becomes unsteady** and so does our breathing. Steadying our breathing relaxes our mind and allows the storm of thoughts to pass. Fewer thoughts mean less distractions and more attention.

Staying Hydrated

Our body depends on water to survive and it is the most essential element for the complete well-being of our body as well as our mind. Dehydration doesn't just affect our bodily functions, it affects our attention span too. As per a study conducted at the University of Barcelona, mild dehydration—as little as 2 per cent—can negatively impact your ability to concentrate. A point of concern here is that dehydration of such small measure won't make you feel thirsty. That means your attention is suffering without your even knowing about it. So before you take up a task that requires complete attention, make sure you are well hydrated.

Writing over Typing

It is strongly recommended that you take notes in a lecture, meeting or conference using a pen and a paper rather than on a laptop. Researchers at Princeton and UCLA found that when students took notes by hand, they listened more actively and were able to identify important concepts. Laptops are also a source of distraction as you may feel tempted to check emails or your social media accounts. As per Pam Mueller, co-author of the study, 'It may be that longhand note-takers engage in more processing than laptop note-takers, thus selecting more important information to include in their notes.'

Creating a To-Do List of Your Distractions

Whenever your mind wanders away from the task at hand, make a note of the distraction in a notebook and bring your attention back to the task at hand. Firstly, you save a lot of mental energy because you are not engaging in the distraction anymore. Secondly, noting down your distraction will help you decide later whether or not you actually want to go back to the distraction.

Sitting Still

Try to sit still in a comfortable chair in a relaxed position for as long as you can. Make sure that there are no voluntary muscle movements. You will realize, it is not as easy as it seems. You may begin by keeping a target of two or three minutes of sitting still. Once you are able to achieve that target, increase it to five to ten minutes, and then to fifteen. Do not strain yourself at any point and be completely relaxed.

French mathematician, writer and philosopher Blaise Pascal said, 'All of humanity's problems stem from man's inability to sit quietly in a room alone.' We are so used to running around and getting distracted from one thing to the other that we have lost the ability to sit still. Once you practise this activity, you will gain control over your body and mind, which will lead to focused attention on the relevant tasks.[1]

Finger Gazing

Sit straight in a chair, with your head up, chin out and shoulders back. Raise your right arm and bring it to the level of your

---

[1] Brett and Kate McKay, '12 Concentration Exercises from 1918', Artofmanliness.com, 8 August 2012, https://www.artofmanliness. com/articles/12-concentration-exercises-from-1918/

shoulders, pointing to your right. Look around, and moving only your head, fix your gaze on the fingers of the outstretched hand. Keep the arm perfectly still for one minute as you stare at the fingers. Repeat the same exercise with your left arm. Once you are able to do this for one minute, keep increasing the time until you are able to do this for five minutes with each arm. The easiest position is when your palm is turned downwards. If you keep your eyes fixed on your fingertips, you will be able to tell if you are keeping your arm perfectly still.

This exercise requires focus on keeping the body parts still and thus developing better control over them. Such practices help improving your attention span and thus concentration.[2]

Fixing Your Gaze at a Glass Full of Water

---

[2]   Brett Brett and McKay, '12 Concentration Exercises from 1918'.

Hold a small glass of water in your hand. Stretch your arm out directly in front of you. Now fix your gaze on the glass and try to keep the arm steady. You can repeat the exercise with the other arm. Start doing this activity by holding each arm for one minute and then slowly increasing to five minutes.

The idea of doing such practices is to help you control your thoughts and develop a habit of staying focused on one task at a time. So, practising these different exercises helps you to attain better concentration and sharpens the mind.

As mentioned earlier, we are good at distractions as we practise being distracted all the time. Now that our aim is to *improve our concentration*, it becomes imperative that we practise concentration as much as we can. These exercises will play an important part in taking you closer to your goal of reaching a higher state of concentration. They will help you in gaining control over your muscular movements and the rest of your body. As you become better and better, you would be able to control your thoughts and lead them wherever you want. With enough practice and determination, you will truly become the master of your own mind, rather than the other way round.

Summary

- Concentration is not just about connecting your mental and physical energies to one task, but also about disconnecting from the things not relevant to the task.
- Wherever your attention goes, energy flows; wherever energy flows, life grows.
- Paying attention is like giving a slice of your life. So be careful while choosing whom and what you pay attention to.
- If paying *attention* to something is like a beam of light from a torch in the dark, then your choosing which object to throw light on, is the act of *focusing*. Staying with that chosen object for a long time without getting distracted is *concentration*.
- Your perception is your reality; and your perception is governed by your attention.
- Brain is a fantastic filter and attention is its gate.
- No new learning can stick inside the brain without the glue of attention.
- The single most important weapon that each one of us has to shape our life is attention.

- Paying attention to your relationships improves them drastically in positive ways.
- Attention physically changes the brain.
- If you repeat a particular task again and again, this repetition strengthens the neural circuits corresponding to that activity.
- The brain provides the necessary biological infrastructure in the form of *neuroplasticity*. How you harness its power is in your hands, because *you are the master of your attention.*
- Focusing on things that are out of our control only brings us sorrow.
- Your brain cannot multitask. So do only *one* task at a time.
- What you pay attention to and how you pay attention becomes your experience, and by extension, life.
- Whichever 'free' social media platform you use— Facebook, Twitter, LinkedIn, Youtube, etc.—it is not actually free. You are 'paying' in the form of your attention . . .
- The way you talk to yourself about a situation internally, greatly affects the way you cope with it externally.
- A question if asked in the correct way can direct our attention straight to the solutions, whereas the same question asked in a different way can be disempowering.
- Visualization is the property of the brain that can be harnessed to improve concentration and attention by visualizing certainty, by visualizing success and so on . . .
- Over-consumption of a 'high-calorie' digital diet from the Internet can affect your brain.
- Accessible Data + Affordable Data = Loads of Digital Calories

- Distractions may not necessarily be your fault, but managing them is your responsibility.
- A distracted and constantly stimulated brain is a weak and stressed brain.
- Remember: Distraction is *slow* destruction.
- Social media is like a deep ocean where you only see the surface.
- Don't use online platforms to impress people, use it to impact people.
- If attention is the gun, then intention is the direction in which you point that gun. And meditation helps you decide that direction.
- Meditation is attention training.
- Meditation helps develop non-judgemental awareness and improves your decision-making.
- You are the *master* of your attention and concentration. They can be *learnt* with practice.

A Note about the Authors

Aditi and Sudhir Singhal are the founders of Dynamic Minds Group, an organization that works to impart education as edutainment.

They are both maths educators, international memory trainers, authors and motivational speakers. They have to their credit the Guinness World Record for teaching the largest maths class.

Aditi has three records in *The Limca Book of Records* for memory and fastest calculation. *The Limca Book of Records* also awarded her the title of 'Best Memory Trainer'. She is one of the experts on the television programme *Hum Honge Kamyaab*, which focuses on value-based solutions to the problems faced by the youth.

The authors' mantra is: '*Add Smart Work to Your Hard Work*'. *

They can be contacted here:
Email: mvedica@gmail.com;
Website: www.aditisinghal.com
YouTube Channel: www.youtube.com/aditisinghal

/aditieducator   # aditieducator   @aditieducator
/sudhireducator   # sudhireducator   @sudhireducator

Bala Kishore is vice president—transformation, at Searce Technologies. He is a British Chevening scholar, a certified executive coach and digital wellness expert.

Bala is an avid meditator, who practises Raja Yoga meditation, as taught by Brahma Kumaris, for the past quarter of a century.

He has toured sixteen countries to deliver talks on mind, meditation, management and motivation. He is also the co-founder of 'Spirituality in IT' wellness retreats (https://bkitwing.org/sit) and SPIR-IT Summit wellness conference (https://www.spiritsummit.org).

You can read more about him at https://balakishore.in.